THE CATERPILLAR CENTURY

Eric C. Orlemann

MOTORBOOKS
INTERNATIONAL

This edition first published in 2003 by Motorbooks International, an imprint of
MBI Publishing Company, Galtier Plaza, Suite 200, 380 Jackson Street, St. Paul, MN
55101-3885 USA

© Eric C. Orlemann, 2003

All rights reserved. With the exception of quoting brief passages for the
purposes of review, no part of this publication may be reproduced without prior
written permission from the Publisher.

The information in this book is true and complete to the best of our knowledge.
All recommendations are made without any guarantee on the part of the author
or Publisher, who also disclaim any liability incurred in connection with the use
of this data or specific details.

Motorbooks International titles are also available at discounts in bulk quantity for
industrial or sales-promotional use. For details write to Special Sales Manager at
Motorbooks International Wholesalers & Distributors, Galtier Plaza, Suite 200,
380 Jackson Street, St. Paul, MN 55101-3885 USA.

Challenger® and Mobile-Trac System® are registered trademarks of Caterpillar Inc.

ISBN 0-7603-1882-4

Frontispiece: Eric C. Orlemann photo
Title Page: Courtesy of Caterpillar Inc. Corporate Archives

Edited by Steve Gansen
Cover designed by Stephanie Michaud
Interior designed by Mandy Iverson

Printed in Hong Kong

CONTENTS

ACKNOWLEDGMENTS	6
FOREWORD	7
CHAPTER 1 **BIRTH OF A LEGEND**	8
CHAPTER 2 **THE BEST AND HOLT YEARS**	22
CHAPTER 3 **DIESEL POWER**	80
CHAPTER 4 **EARTHMOVER REVOLUTION**	116
CHAPTER 5 **HIGHER HORSEPOWER**	172
CHAPTER 6 **BIGGER AND BETTER**	194
CHAPTER 7 **DIVERSITY AND DRIVE**	242
CHAPTER 8 **GIANTS OF THE INDUSTRY**	278
CHAPTER 9 **A NEW GENERATION**	298
CHAPTER 10 **THE NEXT CENTURY**	360
INDEX	383

ACKNOWLEDGMENTS

A book of this nature, concerning the greatest Caterpillar equipment ever built, would have been impossible without the cooperation of Caterpillar Inc. of Peoria, Illinois. I would like to personally thank the following individuals, both currently employed by and retired from Caterpillar, without whose help and guidance, this project would not have been possible. They are: Mark A. Jostes, Nicole Thaxton, Jeff Hawkinson, Sharon L. Holling, Lea McCall, Ron Nusbaum, Pete J. Holman, and John Ingle.

For the help in obtaining new images of historic Best, Holt, and Caterpillar machinery, I thank the following individuals for granting Nick and me access to photograph their tractors, both at rest and at work, and to the individuals that assisted in the set-up of these treasures. They are: Brent Smith of Oregon; Keith Clark and John Ives of Washington; George E. Logue of Pennsylvania; Ed Akin of California; Allen F. Anderson of Oregon; Don Dougherty of California; Bill Santos of California; Carson Wiley of California; Howard Bowers of Ohio; Kent Bates of Illinois; Peter M. Holt of Texas; Tom Novak of Ohio; and Max Tyler (deceased), Paul Tyler, and Mike Tyler of Montana.

For the people that helped me find the machines, and make the process of setting up photo sessions and verifying historical information a lot easier, I would like to thank Eileen Grafton of Peterson Tractor Co.; Ted Halton of the Halton Company; and Tom Osborne of Wyoming.

Last, but not least, I would like to acknowledge Lorry Dunning and the Joseph A. Heidrick, Sr. Foundation, Davis, California; the Fred Heidrick Jr. Heidrick Ag History Center, Woodland, California; caption writers Curt Bennink of Arizona and Scott Webb of Wisconsin; and photographer Urs Peyer of Switzerland, for their unselfish help in making this project all that it could be. I thank you all.

Eric C. Orlemann
Decatur, Illinois 2003

FOREWORD

When looking at a book that covers a century of earth moving equipment developments, the physical changes are clear. Today's machines are bigger, more operator-friendly and have the ability to be many times more productive than their predecessors.

What is not so outwardly obvious is likely the greatest contributor to equipment advances over the past 100 years — *technology*. The "Caterpillar" track-tractor brought into practical use by Benjamin Holt in 1904 was a technological revolution of its day. The design was adapted to facilitate massive road building projects and major infrastructure projects like dams, canals and waterways. The same technology continues to evolve for use in everything from landscaping applications to housing developments to the building of a transportation tunnel through the Alps. Machine technology also plays a key role in environmental and social improvements like reduced engine emissions and sustainable logging efforts in forests around the world.

While Holt and Daniel Best were the early innovators of Caterpillar equipment, they never could have dreamed of the advances that awaited their crawler tractor. Could they have pictured a day when machine location and condition would be tracked by satellites orbiting high above the Earth? Did they envision a mining machine that would "coach" its operator toward improved productivity through the use of on-board computer graphics?

And what do today's innovators imagine for the *next* 100 years? Will tomorrow's equipment effortlessly hover above the earth it intends to move? Might maintenance some day be performed in real-time by an on-board, holographic, virtual service representative? Will the operator of the future be in the same location, or even the same country, as the fleet of machines he or she controls? Whatever the next technological revolution in equipment might be, you can be assured that Caterpillar people will be at the forefront of helping customers work better, faster and smarter. We're proud of Caterpillar's rich history of innovation, and dedicated to the research and development that keeps us on the forefront of making progress possible.

Glen Barton, Chairman and Chief Executive Officer
Caterpillar Inc.

"Plowing and harvesting by steam a success," said an 1889 advertisement from the Daniel Best Agricultural Works, San Leandro, California, trying to encourage skeptical farmers. Dan Best had purchased the rights to the Remington Traction Engine or Steam Plow; he then improved it and used it to pull a combine of his own design. The Best Traction Engine and the Best Combine Harvester, shown here working together, were first paired as a working team in 1889.
Author's Collection

CHAPTER 1
THE BIRTH OF A LEGEND

Caterpillar's rich heritage actually extends as far back as 1870, when one of its founders, Daniel Best, put his first portable grain cleaner to work in California. From then on, it was innovation after innovation that propelled Best and Caterpillar's other founding member, Benjamin Holt, into agricultural, and eventually earthmoving, history.

It seems that the tracked crawler tractor has been with us forever. This innovation is another one of our fabulous mechanical creations from the twentieth century. All mass-produced tracked machines—agricultural, construction, or military—owe a debt to Holt's first experimental steam crawler from late 1904. In all the accounts of important mechanical achievements of the last century, no credit has really been given to the crawler tractor and its mechanical earthmoving relatives. If you were to believe everything you see on television, then you would have no idea as to the importance these machines have made our everyday lives.

The creations of Best, Holt, and ultimately Caterpillar, have played key roles in almost all of our industrial advancements over the last century. Automobiles would not be what they are if there weren't good roads to drive them on. Airplanes could not land without runways. From giant skyscrapers to massive dams, it all had to start somewhere. Chances are you would find Caterpillar equipment in one form or another laying the groundwork for these projects. It is hard to imagine our current lifestyles without them. Earthmoving and agricultural equipment, such as that built by Caterpillar, makes the world go 'round. Almost everything in our modern society starts with these machines.

A Fortune 100 company, Caterpillar is the world's leading manufacturer of construction and mining equipment, diesel and natural gas engines and industrial gas turbines. The company is a technology leader in construction, transportation, mining, forestry, energy, logistics, electronics, financing, and electric power generation. Its customer service and dealership network are envied throughout the industry. But staying number one is not easy. Caterpillar leads in almost every major equipment category, but it can never sit back on its laurels. Each of its product lines is in competition with possibly dozens of competing companies, some specializing only in one particular type of machine. This keeps the pressure on Caterpillar, but competition also helps Caterpillar produce the best products for its customers.

By 1886, both Benjamin Holt and Daniel Best were building and making their own innovative combined harvesters, and other agricultural machinery to meet the needs of California farmers. As

In 1869, Daniel Best went to work at his older brother Henry's ranch in Marysville, California, and in April 1871 he earned a patent for a portable grain cleaner he developed at the ranch. By 1885, he had added combined harvesters—machines that combined the processes of harvesting, cleaning, and bagging in one unit—to his product line. In 1886, he moved to a larger manufacturing plant in San Leandro, California, which he named the Daniel Best Agricultural Works. In 1888, Best saw a steam traction engine demonstrated and purchased the rights to build it on the West Coast.
Courtesy of Caterpillar Inc. Corporate Archives

they grew in function and power, Best and Holt's harvesters, along with other makes, were getting quite large. They were so large, in fact, that the horse teams could barely pull them through the fields.

The solution to this problem, a new power source in steam, literally drove by Best's office windows in 1888. That spring, a steam traction engine designed by Marquis De Lafayette Remington, a blacksmith, was in San Leandro for a local demonstration. Best was so impressed with what Remington called the Rough and Ready, he purchased the rights to build the 30-horsepower traction engine and sell it on the West Coast, with an agreement that he would not market it in Remington's home state of Oregon. After purchasing the rights to the Rough and Ready, Best immediately started to combine his new steam traction engine with his combine harvester. By February 8, 1889, the first Best traction engine was ready for shipping. It marked the dawning of high-production mechanized farming and the beginning of the end for large horse and mule teams.

Meanwhile, Holt had gone in only four years from building a combined harvester that utilized chains and sprockets instead of conventional belt-driven pulleys to developing a steam traction engine of his own design. Nicknamed "Old Betsy," his first steam-powered traction engine, which he unveiled in 1890, featured steering clutches, something the other manufacturers of the time did not offer. His innovation of disengaging power to one driving wheel or the other earned him another patent in 1893.

Heading into the twentieth century, both Holt and Best offered steam traction engines, matched up to combine harvesters of their own designs. Popular models for Holt included the 40-horsepower Junior Road Engine, the 60-horsepower Standard Road Engine, and the powerful 70-horsepower Senior Road Engine. Popular Best models included a 50-horsepower traction engine from 1889, and a 110-horespower model from 1897. Both the Holt and the Best traction engines were commonly referred to as "steamers."

Even though the Holt and Best model lines mirrored each other almost product for product, customers clearly had their favorites. In the field, the Best steamers were more popular because of their more powerful engines. As for the combine harvesters, the Holt models were by far the most widely used.

The Best and Holt steam traction engines worked well when the going was on dry and stable ground. But in peat or other soft soils, these tremendously heavy steamers would become mired down. A temporary solution to this problem was fitting extremely wide rim extensions, which provided

In 1883, Benjamin Holt moved to Stockton, California, to oversee operations of the Stockton Wheel Company with his brother Charles. Their interest soon expanded to agricultural implements, and they developed an innovative and reliable combined harvester that used chains and sprockets instead of gears. Benjamin soon took a serious interest in steam traction engines and unveiled a steam traction engine of his own design in 1890. In 1892 the company split into two companies: Holt Bros., with Charles as president, and The Holt Manufacturing Company, with Benjamin as president, to reflect an expanding product range and the brothers' different interests.
Courtesy of Caterpillar Inc. Corporate Archives

Daniel Best built combine harvesters, such as this one, to be pulled by teams of horses. One of the hazards of horse-pulled combines was the danger of spooked, runaway teams. One of the selling points of Best's machine was its fan governor, which could absorb the power of the small herd of horses shown in this picture's foreground, even if pulling in a panic.

Courtesy of Caterpillar Inc. Corporate Archives

better flotation. Both Best and Holt used these on their traction engines, but the solution still left a lot to be desired. Another technical breakthrough would be needed to solve this problem. That solution would be the introduction of the belted crawler track.

Though Benjamin Holt did not necessarily come up with the concept of a tracked machine, he was responsible for putting the concept into full production as a completely workable tractor. Inspired by the early designs of the Lombard Log Hauler, Holt went to work on his own creation. On November 24, 1904, Holt started testing a modified version of the Holt Junior Steam Traction Engine No. 77 in the Mormon Slough, near the Stockton city limits. The No. 77 steamer's rear drive wheels had been removed, and in their place was a set of tracks made from malleable link belts with wooden blocks attached to act as treads. Early tests were very encouraging. The tracked steamer was run on soft ground to see if the system would successfully provide enough floatation for the heavy unit. It did.

The competition between Holt and Best finally came to a head in 1905, when Best filed a lawsuit against Holt for patent infringement concerning the design concept of the "power take-off." The case went back and forth in the courts through most of 1906 and 1907. But before a final ruling could be made, Best and Holt agreed to settle the dispute outside the courtroom, and they started talks on the feasibility of combining their companies. On October 8, 1908, Best sold his business to Benjamin Holt, but not before making sure that his son, Clarence Leo Best, would be the superintendent of The Holt Manufacturing Company's San Leandro facility. It was a key position.

The first Best steam traction engine was ready for shipping in February 1889. The Best steam traction engines were very innovative, with vertical boilers and a single front wheel. These machines weighed a hefty 11 tons.
Lorry Dunning Collection

A LEGEND IS BORN

THE CATERPILLAR NAME IS BORN

Benjamin Holt did not invent the tracked machine, but he did put the first workable tracked machine into production. This is the Holt Junior Steam Traction Engine No. 77 with its second experimental track system in March 1905 with Pliny Holt at the controls. In November 1904, Benjamin Holt had begun testing a modified version of his steam-driven, wheel-type Junior Steam Traction Engine No. 77. When he tried replacing the rear wheels with a set of tracks and found that it worked, the future of tracked heavy equipment opened before him. *Courtesy of Caterpillar Inc. Corporate Archives*

Further testing in March 1905 of Holt's No. 77 wheel-type junior steam traction engine, modified with a set of tracks, led Charles Clements, a company photographer often used by Holt, to call the machine a "Caterpillar." Clements coined the term the first time he saw the machine, which amazed him greatly, in action at the Holt family's ranch 10 miles west of Stockton. In a letter written a decade later, Clements described the fateful day he first used the name that would be synonymous with tractors and earthmoving equipment for decades to come:

> Nearing the Holt Ranch, we [Clements, along with Benjamin Holt and P. E. Holt] perceived a steam traction engine in the distance. Mr. Benj. Holt stated — "They are not running." Noticing the absence of the big side wheels, I said — "They are broken down," at which Mr. P. E. Holt turned around, looked at me and laughed, but said nothing. Suddenly I noticed that the outfit was moving along, but did not say anything, thinking that the engine was on board a barge going through some canal, seemingly hidden by the heavy crop of volunteer barley. . . . suddenly it came around between us and the crop of barley, and for a moment I was struck dumb with amazement. Jumping upon my feet I exclaimed aloud — "IF THAT DON'T LOOK LIKE A MONSTER CATERPILLAR." Mr. Benj. Holt reddened at the remark and smilingly asked — "What makes you think that?" I answered — "Why, even a child could make no mistake. Just watch the undulating movement as it creeps along. . . ."

After developing the photos of the tractor, which ran quite slack because the undulation was 12 inches or more when running on wooden slats, Clements placed the pictures in envelopes and marked the name "CATERPILLAR" on them. When P. E. Holt came in looking for the prints of a "platform wheel engine" two days later, Clements did not understand what he meant. After Clements said that he was confused, Holt said, "Why, you photographed the engine day before yesterday at the Ranch."

"Oh! you mean the CATERPILLAR," Clements remarked. "Well," he stated, "whatever you call it, give me three prints as soon as possible."

The name stuck and soon graced the machines that filled farmlands throughout the West Coast. In 1910, "Caterpillar" became officially registered as a Holt company trademark.

A later version of Benjamin Holt's experimental track system is pictured here in 1905. Note the wooden treads bolted to link chains in each track. Holt put clutches on each track to facilitate turning—by engaging the clutch of the inside track, turning the front wheel and powering the outside track, the 20-ton beast would come about.

Courtesy of Caterpillar Inc. Corporate Archives

Around the turn of the twentieth century, Holt offered several steam traction engine models, such as this Holt Steamer Road Engine. As is clear from this picture, the machines did just fine on wheels when the footing was solid and had plenty of horsepower—ranging from 40 on the Junior Road Engine to 70 on the Senior Road Engine. *Author's Collection*

This is the original Holt Junior Steam Traction Engine No. 77 built by, as is visible on the machine, The Holt Manufacturing Company of Stockton, California. Its ultrawide wheels provided a little better floatation, but its field traction still wasn't what was needed. This picture was taken in 1903, as Holt was headed back to the drawing board.
Courtesy of Caterpillar Inc. Corporate Archives

The Best 110-horsepower steam traction engine was introduced in 1897. This steam-powered behemoth helped signal the beginning of mechanized agriculture. Including the 50-horsepower version, Best sold 1,351 steam traction engines by 1912. The pictured Best 110-horsepower Steam Traction Engine No. 175 has been restored to operational condition. There are only about 12 left in various states of restoration.
Lorry Dunning Collection

This is the Best 110-horsepower Steam Traction Engine No. 175, built in 1906. It is equipped with a wide wheel option and is one of only a couple of fully restored and operable examples left.
Nick Cedar

1924: A rare opportunity to compare the Holt 2-Ton, 5-Ton, and 10-Ton tractors side-by-side. These were mainstays of the Holt line, brought over to the new Caterpillar Tractor Co. in the merger the following year. As the new company rationalized its merged product line, even some successful products were discarded to eliminate internal competition. The Holt 10-Ton was the first to go in favor of the Sixty. Then, in 1926, the 5-Ton was eliminated to make more room for the Caterpillar Thirty. Finally, the 2-Ton was replaced in 1928 by the Caterpillar Ten.
Courtesy of Caterpillar Inc. Corporate Archives

CHAPTER 2
THE BEST AND HOLT YEARS

The Holt Caterpillar Model 45 shown here in a 1919 photo was nicknamed "muley." New tractors designed without the front tiller wheel were nicknamed muleys from a farmers' term for a cow without horns. During this period, tractors were competing head to head with four-legged farmhands for work. In an advertisement at the time, Holt summed up the argument for his mechanical Caterpillar Model 45 muley: "It costs nothing when not in actual use. It will replace teams and do more work at less expense."
Courtesy of Caterpillar Inc. Corporate Archives

Another technological advancement contemporary with the development of the track concept was the gasoline engine. Holt had prototyped a gasoline-powered crawler tractor in late 1906. In early 1908, he had built a second unit. Later in that same year, the third tracked gas tractor, a model Holt 40 (Serial No. 1003), was shipped to a paying customer, making it the first gas "Caterpillar" tractor sold. The 40 line first featured tractors that were powered by a four-cylinder, gas valve-in-head motor, with a 6x8-inch bore and stroke, rated at 25 horsepower. Later units of this line were powered by a four-cylinder, gas valve-in-head motor with a 7x8-inch bore and stroke.

The success of the Holt 40 led directly to the Holt 45 series in 1909. Looking much like the earlier 40 tractors, the 45 models were equipped with a different four-cylinder, 6½x8-inch bore and stroke engine. The 45 series tractors were primarily built at the Stockton plant. But two Northern Holt 45Bs, with special twin steering front wheels, were built in 1909 by Benjamin Holt's nephew, Pliny E. Holt, at a subsidiary company, the Northern Holt Company, located in Minneapolis, Minnesota.

While Pliny Holt was in Minneapolis, he had heard of a factory bankruptcy of the Colean Manufacturing Company, located in East Peoria, Illinois. Pliny knew the East Peoria location would be perfect for the production of Holt machinery. On October 25, 1909, a deal was reached that would establish Peoria as another manufacturing location for The Holt Manufacturing Company. The new subsidiary was incorporated in Illinois in January 1910, and it began producing Holt 45 tractors under Pliny Holt's direction.

Just as things were taking off in Peoria, C. L. Best, who was still at Holt's San Leandro facility, was finding it hard to get his ideas approved by the Holt family-controlled board of directors for the company. Best decided that a change was in order. If Holt was not going to build his ideas, then he was going to build them himself. In 1910, he, along with engineers from the company that were loyal to him, left Holt to start their own company in Elmhurst, California known as the C. L. Best Gas Traction Company. And just like that, the feud between Best and Holt was on again.

The event of C. L. Best leaving Holt in no way hindered the company from introducing fresh new models to its customers. Holt was designing and building more than just large tractors during this time period; the company also built a couple of small tractors, too. These were the Holt Baby 30 and the Model 18 Midget. Both of these tractors were for orchard and vineyard farmers who needed small, highly maneuverable tractors to work in the groves. The Holt Baby 30 was introduced in 1912. It looked like its bigger brothers but was proportioned smaller for its intended use. The Baby

was powered by a Holt four-cylinder, 5¼x6-inch bore and stroke, valve-in-head gas motor. The Holt 18 Midget was released in 1914 with a four-cylinder, 4½x5½-inch bore and stroke, Ell-head motor. Both of these small tractors were considered successes for Holt. Both of these tractor models were built at the Stockton plant.

For customers wanting a bit more power and size, the company offered the Holt 60 Caterpillar. The 60 was built at both Holt plants. In Stockton, it was introduced in 1911 as the Holt 60 (T-7). This model was equipped with a four-cylinder, 7x8-inch bore and stroke, valve-in-head, gas motor. The Peoria machine was known as the Holt 40-60 (T-4) and was also introduced in 1911. The 40-60 was equipped with a Holt gas motor that was the same size as the Stockton machine, but utilized an Ell-head valve design. The 60 series proved to be a popular tractor with customers, and the sales for it were a big improvement from the 45 model line.

This Holt 120, shown here in 1918, was born of a request from the military for a 20-ton, very-heavy-duty artillery tractor to pull the big guns into position. It was Holt's most powerful tiller-wheeled tractor, fitted with a six-cylinder, 2,120 cubic inch-displacement, Holt M-8 gas engine. It weighed 26,500 pounds and had a horsepower rating of 70 at the drawbar—very impressive for a tractor at that time. Holt built 698 120s, nearly all of them, as this picture indicates, for military use. *Author's Collection*

If still more power was needed than the Holt 60 could muster, Holt had just the tractor—the 75. The mighty Holt 75 was the most popular and best selling tiller-wheel-equipped Caterpillar tractor that the company ever made. Its record as a tough farming tractor is well known, but it was also an excellent machine for road-building work. The tractor also found itself in the heat of battle as a heavy artillery prime mover with different military armies in Europe during World War I. The 75 was manufactured at both Holt factories. The first model to be introduced, in 1913, was the Holt 60-75 (A-NVS). This tractor was built in Stockton and was powered by a four-cylinder, 7½x8-inch bore and stroke, valve-in-head, gas engine. Starting in 1916, the big tractor, now referred to as the Holt 75 (T-8), was built at both plants in California and Illinois. Most of the production out of the Peoria plant was destined for military duty, which ended in late 1918. These tractors differed from the Stockton-built models in the design of their cooling systems and track assemblies. The engines were the same in both tractors.

Between 1914 and 1915, the Peoria plant had produced a special run of Holt 75 (T-6) tractors, equipped with a different Holt gas motor. The major design difference between this motor and the one found in the regular 75 was the use of an Ell-head valve layout. The success of this design was rather limited because of engine problems, and only a small number were ever produced.

In 1921, the last Stockton design of the Holt 75 tractor was released with an improved radiator design and upgraded track assemblies. This Holt 75 was still considered a T-8 model series when its time in the product line finally came to an end in 1924.

Largest of all the Holt tiller-wheeled gas powered tractors was its mighty 120. Introduced in 1914, the Holt 120 (A-PEP) was designed for military use as a very heavy-duty artillery tractor. The first series of these impressive machines were powered by a Holt six-cylinder, 7½x8-inch bore and

This is actually a Caterpillar Sixty, despite what is cast into the radiator housing. The tractor was delivered in June 1925, just after the Holt–Best merger deal was put together and the Best 60 became the Caterpillar Sixty. In the massive changeover, castings from the Best 60 were used to put this machine together. *Courtesy of Caterpillar Inc. Corporate Archives*

stroke, "Enclosed" Peoria motor. But problems with this engine led to an improved model in 1915 as the Holt 120 model T-9. The engine carried the same basic configuration as the previous model, but was of an Ell-head design. With its 120 brake-horsepower, most of the 120s were destined for the war in Europe with Great Britan and the United States. All were built in Peoria. In 1922, the model was withdrawn from the product line.

The eventual success of Best's new company relied on the kind of tracked tractor models he would design and put up against Holt's many offerings. Best's first introductions were round-wheel type tractors, powered by husky Buffalo gas engines. Models ranged from approximately 40 to 90 horsepower. In late 1912, Best introduced the company's first tracked, tiller-wheeled, gas-powered machine—the C.L.B. 70-horsepower Tracklayer. Best's 70 Tracklayer incorporated many advanced features not found in the Holt machines, such as power-assisted steering for the front tiller wheel and the liberal use of high-grade steels. The 70 was powered by a Best-designed four-cylinder, 7¾x9-inch bore and stroke gas engine. The 70 was a husky looking machine and proved it was just as tough as its counterpart, the Holt 75. In 1914, the 70 became the 75 Tracklayer. Virtually the same design, the 75 had a little more power to offer. These tractors proved so popular that Best was able to repurchase his father's larger former plant in San Leandro in mid-1916 (Holt had moved its remaining operations out around 1913), which increased his manufacturing output considerably. Production ended on the big Tracklayer in 1919. Though designed as a tracked machine, a small number were built as C.L.B. 75-horsepower "Round-Wheel" tractors. This model was basically the Tracklayer version with its tracks removed and replaced with 90-inch-diameter wheels. Other big Best Tracklayers included the C.L.B. 90 H.P. and the C.L.B. 120 H.P., both in 1916.

So far, all of the tractors built by Holt and Best were steered by a front tiller wheel. The Holt 45 (T-10), the company's first full production tractor that did not require the tiller wheel, was introduced in 1914. The 45 "muley," as it was nicknamed, was powered by a gas, four-cylinder motor, with a 6x7-inch bore and stroke and was rated at 45 brake horsepower. Key to the 45's design was its use of a simple, direct independent drive for each crawler, allowing for independent track control. This design enabled the tractor to turn in its own length, a feat that had been practically impossible for a tiller-wheeled machine. This capability allowed the 45 to work in more confined areas. The 45 proved to be quite a tough tractor out in the field. But the tractor's success there was only part of the story. The Holt 45 would really prove its worth, not in the farming fields of America, but on

The Holt 75 (T-8), pictured here in 1917, was a very popular tractor—the best-selling tiller-wheeled tractor Holt ever made, with sales of 4,626 units overall. It performed as well on the farm as it did building roads and towing 75-millimeter artillery pieces to the battlefield. Holt first produced the T-8 exclusively in Stockton, California, but opened another 75 line in Peoria, Illinois, in 1916. The Peoria versions, like the one in this photo, had slightly different cooling systems and track assemblies from their California brethren. *Courtesy of Caterpillar Inc. Corporate Archives*

This Stockton version of the Holt 75 (T-8), like the Peoria version, had a four-cylinder, Holt M-7 valve-in-head gas engine with a displacement of 1,413 cubic inches. In 1921, an improved design of the Stockton Holt 75 (T-8) was released, with an upgraded radiator and track assembly. The Stockton Holt 75 line was finally shut down in 1924 after an 11-year run.
Courtesy of Caterpillar Inc. Corporate Archives

the battlefields of Europe. Battlefield and supply line conditions called for vehicles that could operate under the most severe conditions imaginable. If you couldn't keep your lines of supply open and your artillery on the move, you were not going to win World War I. The answer to these challenges was the tracked artillery tractor.

In November 1915, the U.S. Army put the Holt 45 through a rigorous testing program at Fort Sill and found that the tractor was up to military duty. Overseas, the French military found the Holt 45 to be an ideal medium-sized artillery tractor and prime mover, as did the U.S. Army. To complement this model of the 45, Holt built a special version known as the Model 45 E-HVS (T-12) Armored Artillery Tractor in 1917. This model differed from the standard 45 in that it was covered in armor plating and had a cast-steel frame. The motor was the same as in the standard unit.

Not long after Holt introduced its first muley (without a tiller wheel) tractor, Best would counter the innovation with a design of its own in late 1914, the C. L. Best 40 Tracklayer. The Best 40 was in direct competition with the Holt 45. Even though the tractor was down five brake-horsepower from the Holt, it made up for the lack in power with its overall lighter working weight. Production on the Best 40 would end in 1919.

By 1919, Best had lost the battle with Holt in the competition to sell machinery to the military. But this would be the year that Best introduced what would become one of the greatest crawler tractor models ever to pull through fertile soil—the Best 60 Tracklayer. The Best 60 marked a significant turning point in the evolution of the crawler tractor. Some of the features that made the 60 model such a standout performer were its oscillating track sections, the use of some 36 antifriction bearings to reduce friction and wear in key mechanical areas, and a steering system that utilized roller-bearing-mounted, multiple-disc enclosed friction clutches. The motor in the tractor was a big four-cylinder Best $6\frac{1}{2}$x$8\frac{1}{2}$-inch bore and stroke, gas engine capable of 35 drawbar-horsepower and 60 belt-horsepower. But by 1922, power output on this model had increased to 40 drawbar-horsepower.

The Best 60 was a reliable and extremely tough tractor out in the field. For its time, this crawler tractor was simply the finest large muley money could buy. In a few years, it would also become the backbone of the Caterpillar Tractor Co.'s new tractor product line, not as a Best 60, but as the legendary Caterpillar Sixty.

The Best 60 pretty much replaced the 40 in the company's crawler tractor lineup. In 1921, Best introduced its 30 Tracklayer. The Best 30 was based on the design principles of the popular 60

model. The 30 was approximately half the size of the 60, both in size and in power. It was equipped with a four-cylinder, Best 4¾ x6½-inch bore and stroke motor, rated at 18 drawbar-horsepower and 30 belt-horsepower. Like the 60, the 30 was one tough little crawler, and it proved to be a very popular tractor in the marketplace.

The smallest tractor in the Holt product line in the early 1920s was the 2-Ton, or Model T-35. Introduced in 1921, the 2-Ton was powered by a four-cylinder, 4x5½-inch bore and stroke motor, rated at 15 drawbar-horsepower and 25 belt-horsepower. The original model used an undercarriage and track frames that were riveted together. In 1924, a new cast-steel fabrication was introduced, which was far stronger than the riveted design. Later that same year, the radiator housing had the "HOLT" name cast on the sides, replacing the previous stencil cutout design.

Next up in size was the Holt 5-Ton (T-11). Orginally introduced in 1917 as the 5-Ton Artillery Tractor Model 1917, the tractor was designed primarly as a military prime mover. Almost all of the production of these tractors was farmed out by Holt to the Maxwell Motor Car Company of Detroit,

Michigan, and the Reo Motor Car Company of Lansing, Michigan. This early T-11 version of the 5-Ton was powered by a four-cylinder, 4⅜x6-inch bore and stroke engine, rated at 40 brake-horsepower. These tractors were unique in that they carried the U.S.A. letters on the radiator fronts, instead of the standard Holt identification. Production would end on the military T-11 tractors in 1918. In 1919, Holt would start to build the T-11 5-Ton as a commercial tractor for more peaceful working endeavors.

In 1921, Holt started the development of an improved 5-Ton tractor identified as the Model T-29. After a series of nine prototype tractors were built and tested, the T-29 was officially released for sale in mid-1923. The early T-29 was designed around an undercarriage track frame that was a riveted fabrication. All of these riveted type were assembled at the Stockton facilites between 1923 and 1924. In late 1924, an improved model called the New 5-Ton Caterpillar Tractor was released. This tractor featured an improved cast-steel frame and was built exclusively at the Peoria facilities.

The largest muley tractor offered by Holt during this time was its 10-Ton model series. This robust Holt tractor like so many of its time, started life as a military offering in the guise of the 10-Ton Model 55 Artillery Tractor. It was produced from 1917 to 1919. Holt built a commercial prototype version of the 10-Ton in 1918, but production would not actually begin until 1919 as the 10-Ton (T-16). All of these models were powered by a four-cylinder, 6½x7-inch bore and stroke engine, rated at 55 brake-horsepower. In 1921, Holt also released a special version of the 10-Ton to compete directly with the Best 60 in the western part of the United States called the Western 10-Ton (TS-21). All of these special Western tractors were built at the Stockton plant.

In many respects, the war in Europe shaped the future for Best and Holt, though neither one knew it at the time. During the years of about 1915 and 1919, almost all of the tractor design and production built by Holt was for some type of military application, with design specifications dictated by the U.S. Ordnance Department. At the time, Holt had no reason to worry, since the company was building tractors in record numbers.

On the other hand, the C. L. Best Gas Traction Co. had obtained assurances from the government that farm-crawler tractor production could continue. Best would supply tractors to farmers, while Holt would see to the military's needs. This arrangement would give Best a distinct advantage in designing and building a tractor that was well suited to work on the farm. The Best 60 and 30 were clear evidence to that. But after the war was over, situations started to arise that neither company was really prepared to deal with on its own.

After the armistice was signed in November 1918, one of the first things to start flowing into Holt's company offices was a stream of canceled tractor orders from the U.S. Ordnance Department. At the beginning of the war, the military had requested 24,791 track-type tractors from Holt and the licensed manufacturers. But by the end of the war, only 9,771 tractors had actually been built and delivered. This shortfall created many internal problems for Holt, since factory war expansions were based on a much larger number of tractors being built.

The Holt 10-Ton was a successful tractor in its own right, but to match the competition from C. L. Best in the western United States, Holt built a special version at its Stockton, California, plant called the Holt Western 10-Ton. Launched in 1921, it was significantly different from the Holt 10-Ton, with an upgraded four-cylinder, 929 cubic inch displacement, Holt M-21 gas engine. Its undercarriage was shorter, with wider tracks to better distribute the load and reduce soil compaction. It was not a success in terms of sales, as only 152 Western 10-Ton tractors were sold.
Author's Collection

The Holt 10-Ton (T-16) tractor, shown here in late 1924, was originally released in 1917 as the 10-Ton Model 55 Artillery Tractor, intended for use on the battlefields of France. The Model 55 was armor-plated, and had a 40-drawbar-horsepower, four-cylinder, Holt M-11 gas engine with a displacement of 929 cubic inches. The Holt 10-Ton was simply a commercial version. The first prototypes were built in 1918, and full production commenced the following year. It wasn't until 1924 that "HOLT" became part of the radiator housing casting, giving the 10-Ton a more civilized appearance. If it looks a bit tankish around the edges, just remember it used to pull howitzers. *Author's Collection*

But there was another problem for Holt. With no more war to fight, the government had no need for new tractors; nor did it need many of the tractors the military already had. The military gave many of these units away to the Bureau of Public Roads. From there, they were shipped throughout the United States. What the government didn't give away, it sold for pennies on the dollar as army surplus. It did not take farmers and contractors long to do the math and start buying the cheap slightly used Holt models. While farmers saved a lot of money on their tractor purchases, Holt lost out in potential sales.

Even though Best didn't have to contend with the factory conversion from military to commercial development, it too was hurt by the flood of used tractors in the marketplace. The company was not large enough to weather the sales downturn that ensued. In the end, both companies decided the only way to survive was to consolidate their operations.

That's what they did on April 15, 1925, when the law firm of Chickering and Gregory of San Francisco filed a five-page document with the Office of Secretary of State of California. Identified as document No. 113767, the Articles of Incorporation of Caterpillar Tractor Co. established the new company and its main purposes: "To manufacture, produce, buy, sell, import, export, or otherwise acquire, dispose of, or deal in tractors, harvesters, machinery, agricultural implements, and vehicles of every kind and character." In the coming months, after approval from both companies' shareholders, the Superior Court of the State of California ordered the voluntary dissolution of the two companies. The names of The Holt Manufacturing Company, and the C. L. Best Tractor Co. would now fade into history. In their place was a single, stronger, combined corporation. That new firm was the Caterpillar Tractor Co.

The company's first order of business was to eliminate duplication between the two former manufacturing entities. The number of employees was reduced, as was the dealer network, since in most major markets, there was a Best and a Holt dealer. Now there would be a need for only one.

After the merger, the newly formed Caterpillar Tractor Co.'s product line consisted of both the Best tractors and the three current offerings from Holt. The Best 60 and 30 would now be referred to as the Caterpillar Sixty and Thirty. The Holt tractors were simply called the Caterpillar 2-Ton, 5-Ton, and 10-Ton. The colors chosen for the company's products would be gray, with red and black trim.

The next step the newly formed company made was to reduce its overall manufacturing costs. One of the first casualties of this process was the Cat 10-Ton tractor. Though reliable and well liked,

it just was not in the same league as the Sixty, the largest tractor in Caterpillar's model line. Since both tractors were essentially competing for the same customers, the 10-Ton would have to go. The Sixty, which was originally only produced at the former Best plant in San Leandro, California, would now also be built at the former Holt plant in Peoria, beginning in late 1925.

The tractors built at the two different plant locations each used specific serial number identifications. The Sixty tractors built in San Leandro started production in 1919 with the number 101A. The units assembled in Peoria were issued a beginning number of PA1.

The Caterpillar Thirty was also produced at the two different plant locations during its life in the product line. The tractors built in San Leandro from 1921 to 1930 carried a beginning serial number

Like the Holt 10-Ton, this Holt 5-Ton was originally designed as a fighting machine, introduced in 1917 as the 5-Ton Artillery Tractor Model 1917. Its motor, a four-cylinder, 25-drawbar-horsepower, Holt M-12 gas engine, displaced 425 cubic inches.

Holt began producing a commercial 5-Ton version, like the one shown here, in 1919, but these found competition in army-surplus models. In addition, the army returned a number of tractors to Holt for commercial conversion after the war. In 1923, Holt introduced the 5-Ton (T-29), with the same motor but a completely restyled look. This tractor was improved and released as the new 5-Ton Caterpillar Tractor (T-29) in 1924. *Author's Collection*

of S1001, while the models assembled in Peoria between 1926 and 1932 began with a number designation of PS1. All of the Thirty tractors were painted in gray with red trim, except for the units produced after December 7, 1931. These were painted Caterpillar Hi-Way Yellow with black trim.

The little Caterpillar 2-Ton was the smallest tractor in the early Caterpillar line, and the longest running of the Holt designs to remain in production. For the most part, this model was left virtually unchanged from late 1924. After the merger, a new casting for the radiator housing was made with the Holt name removed and replaced by the words 2 TON. This model proved to be very popular with orchard and vineyard farmers, which accounts for the rather large number of tractors sold in such a short time. Though this version of the 2-Ton was only produced from 1924 to 1928, some 8,989 units of the little Caterpillar were built.

The 2-Ton was replaced in December 1928 by the Caterpillar Ten (PT) model line. The first full year of production for the Ten is listed as 1929, since only four tractors were indicated as being built in the closing days of 1928. The Cat Ten was powered by a four-cylinder, 3⅜ x4-inch bore and stroke gas motor, rated at 10 drawbar-horsepower and 14 belt-horsepower. By the numbers, the Ten was a bit smaller and less powerful than the 2-Ton. The Ten weighed in at 4,000 pounds, while the old 2-Ton tipped the scales at about 5,300 pounds. A high-clearance model, raising the Ten another 24 inches, was also offered to aid farmers in their row crop work. The Ten was well liked in the marketplace, especially by orchard farmers, who favored the machines because they maneuvered effortlessly between groves of trees. The biggest complaint from the field was its reputation to vapor lock on hot days. Because the fuel tank was mounted on top of the engine, the tank got hot easily and the heat spurred vapor locks, stopping the flow of fuel from the fuel line to the carburetor. It would take Caterpillar engineers a few years to get the message and move the tank away from the top of the engine in future designs.

During these early years of the Caterpillar Tractor Co., there were also three separate lines that were referred to as Model Fifteen tractors—a situation that led to confusion among those not familiar with the company's product line. The first of the Caterpillar Fifteen (PV) tractors was introduced in 1929. The PV series Fifteen tractors were powered by a four-cylinder Cat 3¾x5-inch bore and stroke gas engine, which was rated at 15 drawbar-horsepower and 20 belt-horsepower. Production of the fifteen (PV) would end in 1932.

In 1932, two more models of Caterpillar Fifteen tractors were introduced. These were the little or "small" Fifteen (7C), and the Fifteen High-Clearance (1D). These new Model Fifteens were not the replacement tractors for the discontinued Fifteen (PV) series. Rather, they were the new replacement designs for the Ten (PT) model line. Both of these tractor models were powered by a four-cylinder, Cat 3⅜x4-inch bore and stroke motor rated at 15 drawbar-horsepower and 18 belt-horsepower. The improvements over the old Ten were quite substantial, especially the relocating of the fuel tank from on top of the engine to in front of the operator. The vapor lock problems disappeared and the new placement acted as a firewall. But by now, potential customers of the Fifteen had already moved on to more powerful tractors. Caterpillar quickly realized the change in the marketplace and pulled the plug on both Fifteens in 1933.

The serial number (No. 1004) on this Holt 40 identifies it as the fourth unit built. Built in 1908, this is currently the oldest surviving Holt tracked tractor.
Nick Cedar

In 1927, Caterpillar released its Twenty (L) model line. The Twenty was the first Caterpillar tractor model to be designed and built by the company that did not rely on an older Holt or Best creation. The first Twenty series was built in San Leandro, but starting in 1928, the Twenty (PL) started to come off the Peoria line as well. The engine found in both units was a four-cylinder, 3¾x5-inch bore and stroke, gas motor, rated at 25 belt-horsepower. Twenty L-series tractor would continue to be built in San Leandro until late 1929, with Peoria following in 1932 with the PL type.

In 1932, another Caterpillar tractor carrying the Twenty identification was released. Carrying the serial number identification of 8C, it was often referred to as the "small" Twenty. The 8C Twenty model line was not part of the L and PL Twenty model types, but was instead designed as a replacement for the Fifteen (PV) tractor. Built in Peoria, production would draw to a close at the end of 1933.

One of the best selling of Caterpillar's smaller early gasoline powered tractors was its model Twenty-Two (2F) from 1934. Designed as a replacement for the 8C-series Twenty, the Twenty-Two utilized a four-cylinder, 4x5-inch bore and stroke motor, rated at 28.39 belt-horsepower. In 1937, and improved version of the Twenty-Two (1J) was released into the marketplace, which was available until 1939. The 1J series was basically the same as the 2F types, with most of the improvements revolving around improvements with the manufacturing process of the tractors.

In late 1931, the company introduced the replacement for the old PL-series Twenty in the form of the Twenty-Five (3C). The Twenty-Five utilized the same engine found in the old Twenty, but was rated a bit higher power wise at 35.18 belt-horsepower. Production would cease in 1933 when the model was replaced by the Twenty-Eight (4F). The Twenty-Eight had a larger 4³⁄₁₆x5½-inch bore and stroke motor, rated at 37.47 belt-horsepower. But the production run for the Twenty-Eight would be a brief one ending in 1935. This has more to do with potential customers starting to move away from gasoline powered tractors to diesel powered alternatives instead.

In 1935, a Caterpillar tractor wearing the Thirty designation was once again available in the product line, which had been left vacant since the discontinuation of the old PS-series Thirty in 1932. This new Thirty, carrying the serial number designation of 6G, was powered by a 4¼x5½-inch bore and stroke motor, capable of 41 belt-horsepower. This model of the Thirty would continue on through early 1938, at which time, it was renamed the R-4.

Above: The Aurora Engine Company was established in Stockton, California, in October 1906 to develop gasoline engines for Holt. This resulted in the Holt 40. It was fitted with a four-cylinder gasoline engine with a bore and stroke of 6x8 inches. This valve-in-head motor produced 25 drawbar-horsepower. *Nick Cedar*

THE BEST AND HOLT YEARS

The Holt 40 was the first gasoline crawler tractor sold by Holt. This is Serial No. 1004, which was built in 1908. This first tractor actually sold carried Serial No. 1003. The two tractors that proceeded this unit were never sold for commercial use.
Nick Cedar

THE BEST AND HOLT YEARS

Above: In the first part of this century, crawler tractors such as this 1915 Holt 18 Midget used a tiller wheel at the front to help steer it and support the long frame. The steering wheel drives a worm gear, which rotates the tiller wheel through almost 90 degrees. However, this was only effective for minor directional changes, unless one of the crawlers was disengaged by its respective clutch and then braked for a tighter turn.
Nick Cedar

Left: Early tractors, such as this Holt 40, required long frames to house large-diameter steering clutches, brakes, driveline components, engine, and radiator. The tiller wheel at the front of these tractors served two purposes: it helped support the long frame, and it helped steer the machine.
Nick Cedar

Approximately 747 Best 40 tractors were sold for civilian use between its introduction in 1914 and 1919, when production ceased. The picture shows the first owners of this Best 40 putting it through its paces in the field.
Nick Cedar Collection, Photographer Unknown

A rear-mounted belt pulley came standard on the Best 40. It also featured side curtains that could be rolled down to protect the tractor from exposure to the elements.
Nick Cedar

The Best 60 earned a reputation for reliability in the field. For this reason, it appeared in many configurations, such as the Best 60 Logging Cruiser that had a three-speed transmission geared for a 4-mile-per-hour top speed and the Snow Special that featured an enclosed cab with a heating coil operated from the exhaust, dual mounted front headlights, and an engine hood with canvas curtains on the side.
Nick Cedar

Above: The Best 40 engine had four individually cast cylinders. It produced 40 brake-horsepower. In 1918, a special version of this tractor was produced, the C. L. Best 45. It featured 5 additional horsepower, but records indicate that only one of this model was built.
Nick Cedar

Left: The Best-designed four-cylinder gasoline engine that powered the Best 60/Cat Sixty enjoyed a long production run, from 1919 to 1931. The reliability of this tractor allowed it to break into applications that were not previously mechanized.
Nick Cedar

THE BEST AND HOLT YEARS

This 1921 Best 30 was powered by a four-cylinder Best motor with a bore and stroke of 4⅜x6½ inches. It produced 18 drawbar-horsepower and 30 belt-horsepower at 800 rpm. It was initially equipped with a two-speed transmission. Later versions offered three speeds.
Nick Cedar

The Holt 60 proved to be a popular tractor. Between its introduction in 1911 and the end of production after World War I in 1918, a total of 951 units were sold. This included 691 units of the Stockton (T-7) version and 260 units of the Peoria (T-4) version. Sixty-three of the Holt 60 tractors were used by the military. *Nick Cedar*

THE BEST AND HOLT YEARS

A re-designed Holt 2-Ton (Model T-35) was introduced in June 1924. The initial model used a riveted undercarriage and had the Holt name on the radiator in stencil cutout form. The 1924 version introduced a stronger undercarriage with cast-steel construction. The radiator on these models displayed the Holt name cast on the sides. Note the stenciled *Holt* on this early model's radiator.
Nick Cedar

Above: The Holt 10-Ton Tractors used four-cylinder, Holt M-11 gasoline engines. These power plants were rated at 55 brake-horsepower and 40 drawbar-horsepower. The engine was mated to a three-speed transmission, with different gear ratios available to match the intended applications. *Nick Cedar*

Left: The Holt 10-Ton was introduced after the war based on the success of the company's 10-ton Model 55 Artillery Tractor. The commercial Holt 10-Ton retained the two-part crawler bogey from the army version. It was claimed to result in a better ride at higher speeds and greater ability to cross trenches. The pictured tractor is a 1922 Holt 10-Ton. *Nick Cedar*

Above: A total of 347 Holt 18 Midget tractors were built, all at Stockton, California. This facility was originally the Stockton Wheel Company, founded in 1883. In 1892 the company split into two companies, Holt Bros., with Charles Holt as president, and The Holt Manufacturing Company, with Benjamin Holt as president.
Nick Cedar

Right: The Best 60 evolved over its product life. The first tractors offered a two-speed transmission as standard with an optional three-speed. They weighed approximately 17,500 pounds and the driver sat on a low seat that overhung the rear end. As time passed and power output grew to 4 drawbar-horsepower, a three-speed transmission became standard, weight increased toward 20,500 pounds, and an optional seating position on a solid mount above the fender was added.
Nick Cedar

The 1919 C. L. Best 60 replaced the 40 Tracklayer in the company's lineup. It became very popular due to many innovations, such as an oscillating crawler frame, 36 bearings to reduce friction and wear in key mechanical areas, multiple-disc enclosed steering clutches, and a strong frame that could withstand abuse. This allowed the tractor to expand beyond agricultural applications into logging, mining, and construction.
Nick Cedar

Far Right: A Best-designed, four-cylinder, overhead-valve gasoline engine with a 6½x8½-inch bore and stroke powered the 1919 Best 60. It was rated at 60 belt-horsepower and 35 drawbar-horsepower. This powerplant turned at a very slow 650 rpm, one of the slowest fitted to an early crawler tractor.
Nick Cedar

During the merger in 1925, an inventory of components cast with Best logos and part numbers had to be used up. Therefore, there were a few Cat Sixty tractors sold with the Best name on the radiators. After the merger, this model changed colors from Best black-and-gold to gray-and-red livery.
Nick Cedar

Below: Tractor numbers 1C1 and 1C2 were the only Diesel Sixty Tractors painted gray with no color trim. The machines manufactured in the Peoria plant were painted Hi-Way Yellow, trimmed in black. The only exception might have been 1C3. It was reportedly painted gray with no color trim.
Nick Cedar

Right: The Cat Diesel Sixty, such as the 1931 version pictured, used a Cat D9900 Diesel Engine. This tractor is number 1C2 and was one of only two Diesel Sixty Tractors produced at the San Leandro plant. This is where the design team for Cat's first diesel engine met.
Nick Cedar

Introduced in 1911, the Holt 60 tiller-wheel tractor was built in both Stockton, California, and Peoria, Illinois. The machine built in Stockton was dubbed the T-7 and was powered by a four-cylinder 7x8-inch bore and stroke Holt M-6 engine. The machine built in Peoria was called the Holt 40-60 (T-4) tractor and was powered by a 7x8-inch bore-and-stroke Holt M-3 gas engine with an Ell-head valve design. The pictured tractor is a 1914 Holt 60.
Nick Cedar

The Holt 18 Midget was introduced in 1914. It was the smallest tiller-wheeled tractor built by the company. The pictured tractor is a 1915 model. The Midget's engine was a Holt-designed four-cylinder Ell-head motor with a 4½x5½-inch bore and stroke. The last year for production of this tractor was 1917. *Nick Cedar*

Above: Added to the lineup in 1921, the Best 30 used a design similar to the Best 60 but was approximately half the size. A reputation for reliability made this tractor popular in a number of applications, including agriculture, forestry, and construction.
Nick Cedar

Right: This family portrait shows the Best 25, which was replaced by the Best 30. The Best 30 was closely related in design to the Best 60, but it was approximately half the size. Both the Best 30 and Best 60 eventually became Caterpillar models.
Nick Cedar

The Best 30 could be purchased with either a 43¾-inch track gauge or a 60¾-inch track gauge. Wide shoes could be fitted to the wide-gauge version for work on steep hillsides or soft ground conditions.
Nick Cedar

This is a 1929 Caterpillar Ten with a 44-inch wide-gauge, high-clearance configuration. It was popular for cultivating and row-crop work. Power was supplied by a Caterpillar four-cylinder gas engine with a bore and stroke of $3\frac{3}{8} \times 4$ inches. Various factory extras were available for the high-clearance model, including a canopy, enclosed cab, auxiliary fuel tank, front pull hook, stationary drive unit, and rear power take-off.
Nick Cedar

The C. L. Best 40 was one of the first tillerless tractors manufactured by the C. L. Best Gas Traction Co. Advances in clutch and brake technology meant this tractor could move around without the aid of a tiller wheel.
Nick Cedar

Left: The 40-brake-horsepower C.L. Best 40 Tracklayer was designed to compete with the Holt 45. The Best 40 was a little lighter and it had 5 fewer horsepower. The lighter weight offset the Best 40 and made it stiff competition for the higher horsepower of the Holt 45. *Nick Cedar*

Below: The Best 25 was the smallest tractor built by the C. L. Best Gas Traction Co. It had individually cast cylinders that simplified repair. The 4¾x6½-inch bore and stroke produced 25 belt-horsepower at 800 rpm and 12 drawbar-horsepower. It was essentially a smaller version of the 40 Tracklayer. The pictured tractor is a 1919 Best 25. Three hundred of these tractors were built from 1918 to 1920. *Nick Cedar*

The Holt 2-Ton (T-35) was launched in 1921. At the time, it was the smallest tractor the company produced. It utilized a unique overhead camshaft and produced 15 drawbar-horsepower and 25 belt-horsepower at its rated speed of 1,000 rpm.
Nick Cedar

Far Left: After the Caterpillar Tractor Co. was formed in 1925, the Best 60 became the Caterpillar Sixty. It was very popular, with a total of 18,931 tractors built between 1919 and 1932. The tractors pictured are a 1925 Cat Sixty and a 1919 Best 60.
Nick Cedar

Far Left: In April 1925, the Holt 2-Ton became a Caterpillar 2-Ton. The radiator casting was changed from Holt to read 2 TON, but the tractors were virtually identical. Narrow 38-inch or wide 52-inch track gauges were available. A three-speed transmission permitted speeds of 2.12, 3, and 5.25 miles per hour. *Nick Cedar*

Apart from the revised radiator casting that replaced the Holt name with 2 TON on its sides, the tractor remained unchanged through its life as a Caterpillar tractor. Between its introduction in 1924 and end of production in 1928, a total of 8,989 units were produced. Due to its compact size, it was a popular tractor for farming applications. *Nick Cedar*

"The Greatest Tractive Power of the Age," said a 1917 Holt advertisement for this Model 45 (T-10) "muley." Introduced in 1914, the Holt 45 (T-10) was originally built in Peoria, Illinois. Starting in 1915, production started on the model at the Stockton, California plant as well. This Holt 45 is a 1917 Stockton built machine.
Eric C. Orlemann

THE BEST AND HOLT YEARS

These two Caterpillar Diesel Seventy-Five tractors are pulling 12 cubic yard LeTourneau Carryall scrapers, making fast work of this job. For much of the first half of the twentieth century, LeTourneau scrapers and dozer blades were attached to Caterpillar tractors with great success. In 1935, R. G. LeTourneau brought his company to Peoria, Illinois, to be near the Caterpillar Tractor Co., reducing the time and cost of bringing engine and implement together. In time, however, the two companies became direct competitors. *Author's Collection*

CHAPTER 3
DIESEL POWER

During the late 1920s, Caterpillar research engineers had already started to take a more serious look at the benefits that could be gained from the diesel engine design, as compared to the industry-accepted gas engine. The diesel engine was nothing new, as a prototype of it had been successfully tested by Rudolf Diesel in 1895. But the early uses for the engine had centered around marine and stationary engine utilization. Caterpillar's interest in the engine concept was piqued when a tractor equipped with a Benz diesel engine beat a Caterpillar Sixty gas tractor in an overseas comparative equipment demonstration in 1927, plowing a cotton field in the Gezira Plains of Anglo-Egyptian Sudan. Caterpillar almost immediately purchased one of the Benz diesels and had it shipped to its research department for further inspection. The Benz design was a good one, but Cat felt that if the company was going to develop a diesel engine that was going to perform reliably on a moving tractor out in the elements, it would have to be of Cat's own design.

A young Caterpillar engineer by the name of Arthur "Art" Rosen is probably the man most responsible for the design of the first Cat diesel engine. Working out of the San Leandro plant, Rosen and his team built a prototype four-cylinder diesel testing unit. The information gained from this unit was then applied to the building of full-size production engines. Two test diesels were initially built and placed into Cat Sixty-type crawler chassis. The chassis frames were heavier and reinforced and included a special geared-down version of the transmission used in the gas version. By September 1931, the first of a new breed of Caterpillar tractors, the Diesel Sixty, was ready to be delivered to customers.

The first of the production Diesel Sixty tractors to be sold was unit serial No. 1C2, which was shipped from the San Leandro plant and delivered on September 14, 1931, to the W. C. Schuder farm in Woodland, California. Only the first two Diesel Sixty tractors were built at the older San Leandro plant, and both were painted in the original Caterpillar gray color scheme. Starting with 1C3, the rest of the production run was built at the East Peoria, Illinois, facility. All of these tractors were painted in the new Cat Hi-Way Yellow paint, which was officially made the standard color on December 7, 1931 (by order of J. D. Fletcher, Caterpillar Export Sales Manager, Circular Letter No. 53). But a Cat silver gray, trimmed in black option was also offered at no extra cost to those customers who just couldn't accept a yellow Cat. Tractor 1C3, the first Diesel Sixty to come off the assembly line at the East Peoria plant, was completed in late October and was delivered on November 7, 1931, to Oahu Sugar Company, Waipahu, Oahu, Hawaii.

The main advantages of the diesel engine over a gas unit were its tremendous low-end torque curve and its superior fuel economy. The Cat D9900, four-cylinder, $6\frac{1}{8} \times 9\frac{1}{4}$ -inch bore and stroke engine in the Diesel Sixty was a real stump puller. Maximum power was available over a much wider working range than a gas unit, and the gas engine couldn't touch the diesel when it came to economy of operation. This point was well proven in 1932, when Diesel Sixty 1C12 set a new world's record for nonstop plowing.

Tractor 1C12 was originally delivered on February 29, 1932, to Mark V. Weatherford's Fairview Ranch, located in Arlington, Oregon. Between March 4 and April 27, 1932, the tractor plowed a total

The most famous Caterpillar Diesel tractor ever built was Diesel Sixty (1C12), forever to be known as "Old Tusko." Named after an elephant at the Portland Zoo in Oregon, this tractor set world records for nonstop plowing in March and April of 1932.
Eric C. Orlemann

The age of diesel power at Caterpillar began with this Diesel Sixty, 1C1, which was purchased by the Harm Bros. of Stockton, California, on November 7, 1931, the same year this photo was taken. It had taken 36 years for Rudolf Diesel's prototype engine to find its calling in Caterpillar heavy equipment. This Diesel Sixty, 1C1, and the second one produced, 1C2, were the only two ever made at Caterpillar's San Leandro, California, plant and the only ones painted gray. The rest came out of the East Peoria, Illinois, plant and were painted the familiar yellow.
Courtesy of Caterpillar Inc. Corporate Archives

of 6,880 acres, with a total operating cost of only 7.78 cents an acre. Four impartial judges were there to oversee the testing. Three of the judges were professors of agricultural engineering from Oregon State College, Washington State College, and the University of Idaho. The fourth was a farmer and Caterpillar owner who assisted in the testing procedures. Fred Lewis, a Caterpillar field engineer for the service department, described 1C12 in action during the test from his March 10, 1932, service report as follows: "All plowing is done in high gear, except a few steep pitches in the field, on which it is necessary to shift to second gear. The engine seemed to handle the load with ease, and smoked only slightly when on a steep pitch."

The record-setting 1C12 Diesel would eventually be sold in 1935 to Elwood and Harold Hartfield, also of Arlington. It was during this time that the tractor picked up the nickname "Old Tusko," named after an elephant at the Portland Zoo.

Caterpillar thought that with these early achievements of the Diesel Sixty in 1932, customers would be knocking the door down to get to them. But that was not the case. The Great Depression had taken its toll on the nation's farmers. They were not about to risk what little money they did have on some newly introduced, and in their minds, still unproved diesel-powered tractor creation. And there were problems with the early Cat Diesels—though most of these were due to the inconsistent makeup of diesel fuels across the nation. Many farmers assumed that the early diesels could run on just about anything, which they couldn't. Caterpillar recognized this problem early on and spearheaded researching the formulation of more consistent diesel fuels.

Soon Caterpillar's shared research with some of the major oil producers led to the development of the first detergent multicompound oil, called Delo. But getting the proper distribution for the oil proved rather difficult. A solution was finally found when Caterpillar started supplying single-cylinder test engines to the oil suppliers, so they could fully develop and test lubricants that would eventually be marketed as suitable for use in Caterpillar diesels.

Even with these early problems, the Diesel Sixty was and is one of the most important tractor milestones in Caterpillar history. With no real sheet metal to speak of, the D9900 Diesel Engine was there for all the world to see. The engine layout and dimensions made for a very compact and clean design, especially when viewed from the right side. Mounted on the left side was a small Cat, two-cylinder, gas "pony" motor. This was used to start the big diesel. Once the main engine fired up, the pony engine was disengaged and shut off. As mentioned before, the Diesel Sixty was more than

just a gas Sixty with a diesel engine strapped on. Along with the beefed-up frame, the radiator was modified. Also, a heavy equalizer spring replaced the previous equalizer bar. Tracks were 34-section links, with tandem-type recoil springs on the undercarriage. Power output for the early units was listed in September 1931 with 63 drawbar-horsepower and 75 belt-horsepower. By February 1932, these figures had risen to 68 drawbar-horsepower and 79 belt-horsepower. By the end of the production run in late 1932, power ratings were listed at 70.25 drawbar-horsepower and 83.86 belt-horsepower.

The Caterpillar Fifty was an unusual machine, its exposed engine taking in air for combustion on one side and exhausting it on the other for a cross-flow effect. Its gasoline-powered, four-cylinder Cat 7500G Engine had a displacement of 617 cubic inches and produced just over 50 drawbar-horsepower. Early versions of the Caterpillar Fifty put the gas tank in front of the operator, and then engineers decided to relocate it behind the seat, as can be seen in this 1935 photo of a Fifty pulling a No. 66 Grader.

Author's Collection

But there has always been some controversy over the designation of the 1C diesel tractors. In the beginning, they were referred to as the Diesel Sixty; in the middle of the run they were simply called the Caterpillar Diesel. By the end of the production run, they were known as the Diesel Sixty-Five. There was no discernible break in the serial numbers to indicate what happened where and when. Most of the early models in 1931 had SIXTY cast on the radiator sides, but a couple also had DIESEL cast on the sides. This casting difference happened sporadically in the early part of 1932, before the DIESEL nomenclature was the only casting made.

While the diesel Caterpillar tractors were attracting a lot of attention with their new features, increased power and fuel efficiency, gas engine Caterpillar tractors were not about to go quietly into the night. Caterpillar continued releasing new models, but for the first time in many model lines, the same tractor was offered in both a gas and a diesel version. Mid-sized tractor offerings with dual identities included the Thirty-Five, Forty, and Fifty model lines.

The Caterpillar Thirty-Five (5C) was originally released in a gasoline engined form in 1932, equipped with a Cat 6000G, four-cylinder, 4⅞x6½-inch bore and stroke motor, rated at 41 belt-horsepower. The Diesel Thirty-Five (6E) would follow in 1933 with a Cat D6100, three-cylinder, 5¼x8-inch bore and stroke, diesel engine. It was rated at 46.15 belt-horsepower. Both models would have short production lives, with the Diesel Thirty-Five calling it quits in 1934, followed by the gas version in early 1935.

The Thirty-Five model lines were replaced with the slightly more powerful Forty series. Introduced in 1934, the gas powered Forty (5G) was equipped with a Cat 6500G, four-cylinder, 5⅛x6½-inch bore and stroke engine, rated at 48 belt-horsepower. The Diesel Forty (3G), also released in that same year, got its power from a Cat D6100, three-cylinder, 5¼x8-inch bore and stroke diesel, with a power output of 49 belt-horsepower. Both models would end production in 1936.

The Caterpillar Fifty was released in both gas and diesel engine versions as well. The gas-powered Fifty (5A) released in 1931, had a Cat 7500G four cylinder, 5½ x6½-inch bore and stroke motor, and was initially rated at 55 belt-horsepower. Its alternative-fueled brother, the Diesel Fifty (1E), which wasn't released until 1933, was equipped with a Cat D7700, four-cylinder, 5¼x8-inch bore and stroke, diesel engine, which produced 65.60 belt-horsepower. The Diesel Fifty would end its production run in 1936, followed by the gas version in 1937.

Like other Cat tractors produced in the early 1930s, the Fifty tractor was offered with both diesel and gas engines. With customers voting with their dollars, diesel was starting to look like a winner: The Diesel Fifty sold 2,065 units; the gas-powered Caterpillar Fifty sold 1,808. This Diesel Fifty, shown here pulling a grader, had a four-cylinder Cat D7700 diesel engine with a 5¼-inch bore and an 8-inch stroke. It delivered 56.03 horsepower to the drawbar.
Author's Collection

A Caterpillar Seventy (8D) pulls a No. 66 grader in 1938. The last of the big gasoline-powered tractors, this Caterpillar Seventy was one of 266 produced from 1933 to 1937. It had a 76-drawbar-horsepower Cat 9500G Engine. Despite improvements in diesel fuel production technology, in the early 1930s diesel as a fuel option suffered from exorbitant cost and inconsistent quality. Partly for that reason, Caterpillar made both diesel- and gasoline-powered versions of the Seventy. *Author's Collection*

In 1932, Caterpillar officially introduced the Model Sixty-Five (2D) as the replacement unit for the gas Sixty, the tractor that had really put the company on the map. The Sixty-Five looked nothing like its predecessor. The sheet metal design for this tractor was unique in the Caterpillar lineup, maybe a bit too unique. With its high-mounted and rounded hood and tall-looking radiator, the Sixty-Five looked like a mechanical pachyderm. This metalwork housed a Cat 9000G, four-cylinder, 7x8½-inch bore and stroke gasoline engine, rated at 79 belt-horsepower. The frame and undercarriage of the tractor was based largely on the Diesel Sixty/Sixty-Five design, and was not just a straight carryover from the gas Sixty. The biggest modification was with the shortening of the frame rails for the more compact gas engine installation. The gas Sixty-Five was a solid performer in its brief production life, which ended in mid-1933. The tractor's outside appearance was just too radical of a design departure for its time. Customers basically thought the tractor looked ugly, and who wanted to own an ugly tractor? Today, this model doesn't look all that bad. A bit ungainly, yes, but it is one of the more interesting tractor sheet metal designs in the company's history.

For Caterpillar, the Models Seventy (8D) and Diesel Seventy (3E) would be the starting point for a very successful line of large tractors that would change the way these machines would be perceived in the marketplace. Both of these models were introduced in early 1933, and for the most part used the same sheet metal design, except for different patterns in the hood for air-cleaner and exhaust openings. The real story was, of course, their engines. The gas Seventy utilized a big Cat 9500G, four-cylinder, 7x8½-inch bore and stroke gasoline engine, initially rated at 87 belt-horsepower, which was soon increased to 89.43. The Diesel Seventy was equipped with essentially the same engine found in the original Diesel Sixty tractor, the four-cylinder D9900, but with a little more grunt dialed in, now with 87 belt-horsepower. On paper, both of these tractors looked like sure winners. But the tight money situation in the economy, and ever quickening engineering advances being made by Cat, would quickly take the luster off of the big tractors in the marketplace. Production ended in 1937 signaling the end of the big gasoline engine in large Caterpillar tractors. As for the Diesel Seventy, its time came in 1933, after only a few months of production. You would think by the low production numbers that the Diesel Seventy was a failure. But things are not always what they seem. It was simply time for the tractor platform to evolve, because Caterpillar had a new, more powerful diesel engine design ready to replace its groundbreaking D9900.

Caterpillar started to get serious about large diesel tractors in mid-1933, when it introduced the Diesel Seventy-Five (2E), the replacement for the Diesel Seventy. As large government works projects helped to get America back to work, contractors needed bigger iron to accomplish these big earthmoving contracts. At the same time, R. G. LeTourneau, a builder of tractor equipment attachments and accessories, was introducing larger earthmoving devices, such as pull-scrapers, rooters, and bulldozing blades. The Diesel Seventy-Five was tailor-made to work with these large bulldozer blades and pull-scrapers, and quickly found its place in large production earthmoving and mining operations across the country. Under the hood of the tractor beat the heart of the new Cat D11000, six-cylinder, 5¼x8-inch bore and stroke diesel engine. Power output from this engine was listed at 98.01 belt-horsepower. The new model utilized basically the same undercarriage and track gauge as the Seventy series, though the frame was modified for the installation of the six-cylinder diesel. The Diesel Seventy-Five's run came to an end in 1935.

In 1932, the year this photo was taken, Caterpillar introduced the Sixty-Five, with its distinctive oval hood and imposing radiator (dominant in picture foreground). The frame and undercarriage were based on the Diesel Sixty-Five, but it had a gas-burning, four-cylinder Cat 9000G Engine, rated at 68 drawbar-horsepower. Many today find the old machine beautiful, just as many back in the 1930s thought it looked hideous. It sold just 521 units.

Courtesy of Caterpillar Inc. Corporate Archives

This Cat Diesel Sixty-Five, pictured here in the year of its release, 1932, is pulling a LaPlant-Choate 3-way Dump Wagon. The Diesel Sixty-Five was practically the same tractor as the Diesel Sixty. The same production run began as the Diesel Sixty, continued as simply the Caterpillar Diesel, and ended as the Diesel Sixty-Five. All three tractors utilized an innovative starting, or "pony," motor—a two-cylinder gas motor that was shut off once it got the big diesel going.
Author's Collection

Introduced in 1933 as a replacement for the Cat Diesel Seventy, the Diesel Seventy-Five (2E) helped meet the growing demand for more power at the drawbar. It was based on the same overall design as the Seventy, but with room for a six-cylinder, 5¼-inch bore, 8-inch stroke Cat D11000 diesel rated at 83.23 horsepower. Caterpillar made over 1,000 Seventy-Fives, a good number in those days, by the end of its run in 1935.
Author's Collection

This Caterpillar Diesel Seventy (3E), pictured in 1934, weighed 30,800 pounds and came with essentially the same engine found in the Diesel Sixty-Five, with 76 drawbar-horsepower. At a time when America was deciding whether it liked gas or diesel fuel in its heavy equipment, Caterpillar offered both gas and diesel engines in the Seventy tractor. Both models, the gas-powered Cat Seventy and the Cat Diesel Seventy, were unveiled in 1933.
Author's Collection

Above: The Cat Sixty proved to be one of the most popular tractors built. Of all of the Best 60/Cat Sixty tractors built, 5,415 were manufactured in San Leandro, California, and an additional 13,516 were produced in Peoria, Illinois.
Nick Cedar

Left: Between 1919 and 1931, a total of 18,931 Best 60/Caterpillar Sixty tractors were built. This tractor was built in both San Leandro, California, and Peoria, Illinois. Depending on customer preference, the fuel tank could be mounted on the right side or the left side of the tractor.
Nick Cedar

This Cat D2 Tractor is equipped with orchard fenders, which protect low-hanging fruit trees from damage. It was also available with an optional tail seat configuration.
Nick Cedar

Above: Both the Seventy and the Diesel Seventy were designed with a 78-inch track. The Seventy replaced the Sixty-Five in the company's line-up in 1933, but it was a totally new design that shared nothing with the Sixty-Five.
Nick Cedar

Left: A Caterpillar D7700, which was traditionally used in the Diesel Fifty, was used in the initial conversion of gasoline Best 60/Cat Sixty tractors to diesel in 1933. This was a four-cylinder engine with 5¼x8-inch bore and stroke that produced 63 brake-horsepower.
Nick Cedar

Below: In 1933, Caterpillar offered a diesel-engine conversion for the gasoline-powered Best 60/Cat Sixty tractors. The conversion took approximately 16 to 20 hours for a trained mechanic to complete. There are no records on how many of these conversions took place.
Nick Cedar

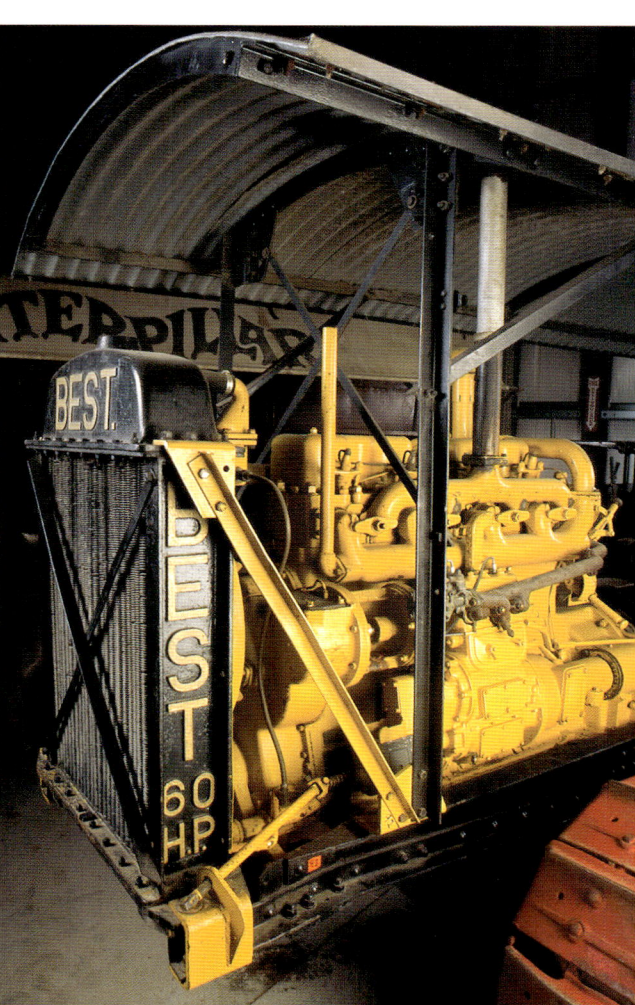

Right: The Seventy introduced in 1933 represented the most powerful gas tractor produced by Caterpillar. Its 9500G four-cylinder engine initially boasted 76 drawbar-horsepower and 87 belt-horsepower. Its ratings were soon increased to 77.07 drawbar-horsepower and 89.43 belt-horsepower.
Nick Cedar

Above: The distinctive exhaust manifold makes it easy to identify this Cat Seventy as a gasoline version. The diesel version of this tractor ranks among the rarest of the large Caterpillar tractors. The Diesel Seventy was only produced in 1933, and only 51 machines were assembled before it was replaced with the Diesel Seventy-Five.
Nick Cedar

Above: Customer input and Caterpillar's previous experience with large tractors were used in the design of the Seventy. But a depressed market kept sales from meeting expectations. While the Seventy was not exactly a sales success, its design set the standard for large tractors that followed.
Nick Cedar

Left: The Seventy and Diesel Seventy used the same sheet metal, except for different allowances in the hood for air cleaner and exhaust pipe openings. They also shared the same 78-inch track gauge and weighed approximately the same, 31,070 and 30,800 pounds respectively. The 1934 Gas Seventy pictured has an optional factory radiator guard.
Nick Cedar

Two hundred sixty-six units of the gasoline-powered version of the Seventy were sold between 1933 and 1937. This sales performance spelled the end of large gas tractor development. But the company did continue to offer smaller gasoline-powered tractors. *Nick Cedar*

Above: The bulk and weight of early diesel engines made them more suited for marine and stationary applications than tractors. The D9900 became the first diesel engine used in a Caterpillar tractor. It powered the Diesel Sixty. This four-cylinder engine displaced a bore and stroke of 6⅛x9¼ inches and was originally rated at 63 drawbar-horsepower and 75 belt-horsepower. A two-cylinder gas pony motor aided starting.
Nick Cedar

Actually weighing slightly more than 10,000 pounds, the Caterpillar 5-Ton (T-29) was one of the few Holt models that made the transition to the new Caterpillar Tractor Co. after the merger in 1925. This picture shows a T-29 version of the 5-Ton with an overhead valve, four-cylinder gas engine displacing 425 cubic inches.
Eric C. Orlemann

DIESEL POWER 111

This gas-powered Caterpillar Twenty (L), shown here in 1929, had a four-cylinder overhead-valve engine running at 1100 rpm and displacing 276 cubic inches. The first Twenty rolled off the line in 1927—the first tractor to do so without Holt or Best ancestors. It was Caterpillar's first complete creation.
Eric C. Orlemann

The Caterpillar Twenty-Five (3C) was the replacement for the Twenty. Production of this model heralded a dramatic change in tractor aesthetics, as these new machines—and every Caterpillar machine since—were painted yellow instead of gray. The vintage model shown is equipped with optional swamp tracks.
Eric C. Orlemann

During the 1930s, diesel tractors became increasingly popular due to low fuel cost and excellent torque characteristics in power delivery. The first Caterpillar diesel tractor model, the Diesel Sixty, was introduced in September 1931. These tractors had a heavier frame than their gasoline-powered counterparts and used a special low-geared transmission. The pictured tractor is a 1C2 built in 1931.
Nick Cedar

Built in 1934 and 1935, this R–3 (5E) tractor was a special order from the United States government. Only 60 units were ever made despite a successful design that was very similar to the Cat Twenty-Eight. Note its "R-3" brand, so distinctive from other Caterpillar trademarks, in the radiator housing in the left foreground.
Eric C. Orlemann

Caterpillar's entry into the pull-scraper market in 1946 allowed the company to perfectly complement its existing tractor line. For instance, the Cat D7 tractor was a perfect match to the No. 70 cable-controlled pull-scraper. Similarly, the No. 40, the smallest of the pull-scrapers, which was hydraulically operated and introduced in 1949, was designed to be pulled by a D4. The No. 60 cable-operated pull-scraper was matched to a D6 and the cable-operated No. 80 was intended to be pulled with a D8. A larger 27 cubic yard heaped capacity No. 90 cable-operated pull-scraper was introduced in 1951, and it was also mated to the D8, which was the largest tractor in the lineup at that time.
Author's Collection

CHAPTER 4
EARTHMOVER REVOLUTION

The Russell Grader Manufacturing Company of Minneapolis, a valuable early acquisition in the Caterpillar mix, built this self-propelled grader, its first, in 1919. It had a single axle, an Allis-Chalmers tractor, and pulled the grader blade behind. The unit was officially unveiled in 1920 as the Russell Motor Hi-Way Patrol. *Courtesy of Caterpillar Inc. Corporate Archives*

While Caterpillar was diversifying the types of engines it offered in the early 1930s, it was also expanding its product line further into the road construction and maintenance market. After buying Russell Grader Manufacturing Company of Minneapolis, Minnesota, in 1928, Caterpillar revamped the Russell line, considered among the best in road maintenance equipment.

After eliminating similar models and models that did not already utilize a Caterpillar tractor, the new product lines consisted of self-propelled, tractor-pulled, and elevating graders. The new Caterpillar self-propelled graders would consist of the Russell company's Ten Motor Patrol incorporating a Cat Ten tractor (1929); the Fifteen Motor Patrol incorporating the Cat Fifteen (1929); and the Twenty Motor Patrol incorporating the Cat Twenty, which was formerly known as a Motor Patrol No. 6 (1928). The last of this design to be released by Caterpillar was the Twenty-Eight Motor Patrol (1933), which utilized a Cat Twenty-Eight tractor. All of these designs relied on a separate tractor model and grader attachment. Caterpillar engineers were quick to realize that it would make far better sense to combine the power tractor unit and the grading mechanism into one cohesive design. This new design would be centered around a tire and wheel drivetrain layout, without the use of any type of crawler track assembly. So was born the Auto Patrol.

Built in 1931, the Caterpillar Auto Patrol was the earthmoving industry's first true rubber-tired, self-propelled motor grader. Unlike the earlier Motor Patrol model lines, where the grader was simply a front-end attachment mounted on an existing crawler unit, the Auto Patrol had its own engine placed high and in the rear of the machine. This placement kept the engine in a cleaner work environment, improved operator visibility, and increased traction on the drive axle. So solid was the design concept, it would form the basis for all motor graders yet to come in the industry. Even today, the basic design layout of the first Auto Patrol is still with us.

While the model was first only called the Auto Patrol, Caterpillar gave it the designation of Model No. 9 late in 1931. In early 1932, a slightly lighter-weight version of the motor grader called the No. 7 was introduced. Production on the No. 9 would end in 1932 and on the No. 7 in early 1933.

Caterpillar was quick to add new and improved Auto Patrols starting with the No. 11 in late 1932. This model was followed by the No. 10 in 1933. Both were gasoline-powered motor graders with a single rear drive axle. Starting in 1934, Caterpillar introduced the Diesel Auto Patrol. Also in that year the company offered tandem-drive rear axles on all of its Auto Patrol models, which helped relieve the

bouncing or "loping" ride that the single rear-axle graders commonly suffered from. Starting in 1937, the Diesel Auto Patrol became the Diesel No. 11, and a Diesel No. 10 version was released in 1936. Both models were available in single or tandem-drive configurations, just as in the gasoline-powered versions. Also in 1935, an option for leaning front wheels was offered for the first time for both model types, an important engineering step in the company's young motor grader lineup.

Mid-1938 would see the release of one of Caterpillar's most significant motor grader designs of all time, the Diesel No. 12 Auto Patrol. Key to the No. 12's success was its triple-box-section main

frame, which was far more rigid and stronger than that of the old twin-beam designs found in previous Auto Patrols. Leaning front wheels were to become stand fare on the No. 12. These wheels made the grader's turns shorter and counteracted side-draft caused by grading forces at the blade. The product line name change began when the gasoline-powered No. 12 Motor Grader was introduced in 1939. But in 1942, the gasoline engine option had been dropped from the lineup. A tandem rear-axle drive layout was the only choice.

At the time of the introduction of the No. 12 Motor Grader, the No. 10, No. 11, Diesel No. 10, and Diesel No. 11 Auto Patrols were still being offered. But by mid-1939 their time had run out, and Caterpillar replaced both model lines with fresh designs identified as the No. 112 and No. 212 Motor Graders. The older Auto Patrol models were still built until the available inventory of their parts was exhausted in early 1940. But after this date, only the newer designs were offered. Both of the new models were basically smaller versions of the No. 12, with the No. 112 being the larger of the two. Each was initially offered in diesel and gas engine configurations, as well as single- and tandem-axle rear drive layouts. By 1947, only the diesel engine mode of power would be available for the two graders.

As the Auto Patrol and diesel engines caught on, fewer gasoline engines sparked interest among buyers. One of the last gas tractor model lines to survive the 1930s and make it into the early 1940s was the "R" series. These tractors were often earmarked for government use, such as various military branches or the forestry service. But many would also find homes in the private sector. Production models of R-series gas-engine models were built at various times between 1934 and 1944, and included such tractors as the R-2, R-3, R-4, and R-5.

The Caterpillar R-2 (5E3501), which was introduced in late 1934, was the first of three different serial-numbered R-2 model lines to be released. The R-2 was powered by a Cat four-cylinder, 4x5-inch bore and stroke gas motor, rated 32.1 belt-horsepower. Production ended on this R-2 model in 1937.

Following the 5E series came the 4J and 6J variations of the R-2 tractor. Based largely on the D2 diesel tractor chassis, the engines were all that differed between the two model lines. Both were powered by Cat 3400G, four-cylinder, 3¾x5-inch bore and stroke gas engines, rated at 31.5 belt-horsepower. Both of these R-2 tractors were built from 1938 to 1942. After this date, no more R-2 tractors were manufactured.

This Caterpillar Ten (PT), even at 4,420 pounds, was the smallest tractor the company made. An upgrade from the Cat Model Twenty, it was displayed for public viewing on September 1, 1928, with production deliveries from Peoria made the following year. It had a four-cylinder, 143 cubic inch displacement gas engine, with a 3⅜x4-inch bore and stroke. The engine was rated at 10 belt-horsepower and 14 drawbar-horsepower. A high-clearance model, like the one pictured here, was offered for the agricultural market. Author's Collection

Acquisition of the Russell Grader Manufacturing Company of Minneapolis in 1928 added valuable grader expertise to Caterpillar. An established leader in equipment manufacturing, Russell had achieved notable success in 1926 with a grader blade mounted in front of a Caterpillar 2-Ton Tractor, known as the Motor Patrol No. 4 (shown here). Its capabilities convinced Caterpillar it was time to bring Russell onboard.

Author's Collection

Between 1934 and 1935, Caterpillar offered an R-3 (5E2501) tractor that closely resembled its Model Twenty-Eight. But the R-3, with its more powerful Cat 5500G, four-cylinder, 4½x5½-inch bore and stroke gas motor, carried a rating of 43.88 belt-horsepower. Most of the R-3 tractors built went to government agencies, especially the forestry service.

The Caterpillar R-4 (6G) was the last of the gas engine tractors to be offered commercially by the company. First introduced in early 1938, the R-4 was actually the Cat Thirty (6G), only with different nomenclature. All mechanicals were virtually the same, including power output. The R-4 model line came to an end in 1944.

Introduced in 1934, the Caterpillar R-5 model lines shared many components with the Cat Thirty-Five and Forty. But the R-5 was not the same as either of these tractors. The R-5 was released in three production batches. The first series, starting with serial number 5E3001, was in production until 1936. In that same year, R-5 units, starting with the serial number 4H501, started production. These lasted until 1940, when the last group, the 3R machines, started rolling off the line. All of the 3R units were assembled in 1940. All three series shared the same Cat 7500G, four-cylinder, 5½x6½-inch bore and stroke gas engine, rated at 64.06 belt-horsepower (64.28 belt starting in 1937).

As the spark-ignition, gasoline-powered Cat engines started to enter their twilight years in the latter part of 1930s, other changes were also taking place that would have significant meaning for the company for years to come. The introduction of the diesel engine and the Auto Patrol were the first steps toward the company's march away from agriculture, at that time its primary market. Soon the company's secondary market, construction and earthmoving equipment, would become its primary focus. Major works programs initiated by the government to help get America out of its worst economic depression and back on its feet increased the demand for heavy construction equipment.

Even though Caterpillar tractors used all sorts of auxiliary equipment, such as bulldozing blades and pull-scrapers, from various allied equipment manufacturers, one supplier stood higher than all the rest. A man and a company by the name of R. G. LeTourneau would help complete the transformation of Caterpillar to the foremost builder and supplier of earthmoving construction and mining equipment in the world. In the earthmoving industry, R. G. LeTourneau was considered one of the foremost experts at producing equipment that could move dirt economically. Products such as his straight and angle dozing blades, power-control units (PCU), Carryall pull-scrapers, rooters, and rock-buggies were used by all of the major track-type tractor builders, including Cletrac, Allis-Chalmers,

and, of course, Caterpillar. But LeTourneau's relationship with Caterpillar tractors would be the one that would really put Caterpillar on the map.

LeTourneau's growing company, with headquarters in Stockton, California, had a good sales force, but it lacked a large dealer network. This would change in 1934, when LeTourneau became an official auxiliary equipment manufacturer for the Caterpillar Tractor Co. With this step, LeTourneau would design equipment specifically for use with and on Caterpillar tractors; in turn, Caterpillar encouraged its dealers to sell LeTourneau's products. This did not include all of the foreign Cat dealer franchises, but many of them also opted for the LeTourneau machines anyway. This agreement did not prohibit Caterpillar dealers from carrying other similarly built allied equipment. But the alliance of Caterpillar and LeTourneau was without a doubt one of the greatest in earthmoving history.

To help in the delivery and production of equipment, LeTourneau enlarged its manufacturing capacity by establishing a large factory in Peoria, Illinois, in 1935. Located in the northeast section

EARTHMOVER REVOLUTION

The industry's first true rubber-tired, self-propelled motor grader, this innovative machine made its debut in 1931. First known simply as the Auto Patrol, it was later designated model No. 9 (8A). Unlike previous machines, which were conglomerations of separate companies' engines and blade attachments, the Auto Patrol was engineered from the ground up as a single unit. Its design has been the basis for every motor grader made since.
Courtesy of Caterpillar Inc. Corporate Archives

of town, it was just down the street and across the Illinois River from East Peoria, the home of Caterpillar tractor. This, of course, was no accident. By having both manufacturers so close to one another, Caterpillar tractors could be shipped directly to LeTourneau for an extremely small fee, then be equipped with bulldozing blades, power-control units, and other attachments, and then be on their way by truck, rail, or ship.

This approach would be of immense importance during World War II, when the government required almost all of the equipment the two companies could produce for the war effort. It was a common sight around the world for service personnel, many of whom had worked for the two companies in peacetime, to be fighting and working side by side with Caterpillar tractors, equipped with bulldozers and pull-scrapers built by R. G. LeTourneau. The machines, and the men who ran them, were truly an unstoppable force. About the only thing that could derail the dominance of the Caterpillar-LeTourneau partnership was the companies themselves, and that's just what happened.

After months of speculation, LeTourneau officially announced in February 1944 that the alliance of the two earthmoving powerhouses was finished. Then in May 1944, Caterpillar announced that it would start producing bulldozers, power-control units, pull-scrapers, and rooters of its own design. Reasons abound for Caterpillar's decision, but one was surely the introduction in 1938 of the Tournapull. The LeTourneau Tournapull was the industry's first true, self-propelled and self-loading, rubber-tired scraper. Even though the Tournapulls were powered by Cat diesel engines, its threat to the company's product line was clear. With every sale of a Tournapull, a possible Caterpillar crawler tractor sale was lost. In 1941, Caterpillar also started to introduce a rubber-tired, high-speed tractor in the form of the DW10, specially designed for scraper and bottom-dump use. It was clear the two companies were now starting to compete with each other, rather than aid each other. If it had not been for the war effort at the time, the agreement between the two companies probably would have ended much earlier than it did.

During the time of its relationship with LeTourneau, Caterpillar diesel crawler tractor development was in high gear. As older gasoline-powered models were retired, new diesel engine models

The Caterpillar Fifteen (PV), shown here in 1930 in a residential setting sporting a Drott Tractor Loader, was a 5,500-pound, gas-powered workhorse. Introduced in 1929, the Fifteen had a four-cylinder, 220 cubic inch displacement engine rated at 15 drawbar-horsepower. It ran at 1,200 rpm and had three gears going forward and one in reverse. Customers had the option of using kerosene in the Fifteen with slight modifications, and could choose between track gauges of 40 and 50 inches. With over 7,500 tractors sold, the Caterpillar Fifteen (PV) was already a very successful machine when two more Fifteen models were introduced in 1932, the "small" Fifteen (7C) and the Fifteen High-Clearance (1D).
Courtesy of Caterpillar Inc. Corporate Archives

were introduced to take their place in the product line. The first of the "small" diesel tractors was the D2. Introduced in 1938, the Cat D2 (3J/5J) continued in the tradition of the company's earlier farming tractors. It was marketed as a small, economical agricultural tractor, as well as a contractor's machine. The D2 was an extremely reliable and thrifty diesel tractor. The 3J and 5J series were powered by a Cat D3400, four-cylinder, 3¾x5-inch bore and stroke, diesel engine, rated at 31.5 belt-horsepower.

In 1947, the D2 (4U/5U) was upgraded with a D311, four-cylinder, 4x5-inch bore and stroke motor, with an increased power output of 38 belt-horsepower. The front radiator housing design was also significantly changed from the previous model. The tough little diesel tractor would remain in the Caterpillar product line all the way up to 1957, at which time the model line was retired.

Next closest in size to the D2 was the RD-4, which was introduced in 1936. The Caterpillar RD-4 (4G) was based heavily on the R-4 spark-ignition gas tractor, but without the engine. The RD-4 was powered by a Cat D4400, four-cylinder, 4¼x5½-inch bore and stroke diesel, producing 41 belt-horsepower. In late 1937, the RD-4 name was changed simply to D4. Everything else with the tractor remained virtually unchanged, except the radiator, which was revised slightly. Other model introductions of the D4 design were the 7J series from 1939 to 1942, the 2T series from 1943 to 1945, and the 5T series from 1945 to 1947. All were powered by the D4400 Diesel. In 1947, a revised D4 (6U/7U) model was introduced equipped with the Cat D315, four-cylinder, 4½x5½-inch bore and stroke diesel, rated at 48 belt-horsepower. Both of these variations on the D4 proved very popular in the marketplace, and with regular updates in horsepower, continued in the product line all the way up to 1959.

In 1939, Caterpillar introduced a model D5 (9M) tractor. Built only in 1939, the D5 featured a Cat D4600, six-cylinder, 4¼x5½-inch bore and stroke, diesel engine, rated at 52 belt-horsepower. The tractor design for the most part was a D6 unit fitted to a special five track roller D4 chassis. After this model was discontinued, the D5 nominclature would not be seen again in the Caterpillar product lineup until 1967.

The Caterpillar RD-6 (5E8501), which was introduced in 1935, was a standout, all-around performer in the product line. This RD-6 model was basically a more powerful version of the Diesel Forty. Only the name was different. But only five units were built with this prefix number, before being replaced by the 2H series in that same year. The new RD-6 was powered by the Cat D6600, three-cylinder, 5¾x8-inch bore and stroke diesel (5¼-inch bore in the 5E series), rated at 51.86 belt-horsepower. In late 1937, the nomenclature of the RD-6 changed to the D6. The appearance of the tractor was unaltered from the original RD-6 model line.

In 1941, an entirely new D6 (4R/5R) model line was introduced. This D6 was a very handsome machine when viewed from any angle. The front end was especially nice, with its rounded edges and tapered lines. This D6 model line was powered by the Cat D4600 Diesel, the same engine as

Although produced after the Auto Patrol No. 9, this version was designated No. 7. It was slightly lighter but retained No. 9's 36.2-horsepower Cat 4200G gas engine. Production of both models ended in 1933, making way for more powerful, diesel-driven motor graders.
Author's Collection

This single-axle Auto Patrol No. 10, introduced in 1933, was actually launched after No. 11 in 1932. The No. 10 was originally a gasoline-powered motor grader. But future models made use of the increased low-end torque and fuel economy offered by diesel engines.

Author's Collection

installed in the original D5 (9M), but with a higher power output of 65 belt-horsepower. The 4R and 5R series of the D6 would continue production until 1947, at which time they were upgraded into the 8U series and the 9U series. Both of these models would stay in the product line until 1959. The big news with these tractors was their use of the Cat D318, six-cylinder, 4½x5½-inch bore and stroke diesel engine, rated at 75 belt-horsepower. Also, the front radiator and hood sheet metal designs were altered from the previous "rounded" look to one that was a bit more conservative.

The Caterpillar RD-7 was everything the RD-6 was, but only in a larger and more powerful form. Introduced in 1935, the first RD-7 (5E7501) model line was essentially a renamed Cat Diesel Fifty with more horsepower. The RD-7 came into its own with the release of the 9G series in late 1935. The 9G series was powered by a Cat D8800, four-cylinder, 5¾x8-inch bore and stroke diesel engine, rated at 70 belt-horsepower. In late 1937, the "R" was dropped from the nomenclature as in previous model lines, and it was now referred simply as the D7. The 9G series was produced until 1940, when it was replaced by the 7M series D7 in that same year. The D7 (7M) would be replaced by a further improved model in 1944 carrying the serial number prefix of 3T. The 3T series would run until 1955, at which time the D7C (17A) would take over. The D7C would in turn be upgraded into the D7D (17A) in 1959.

When the sales agreement with LeTourneau terminated in 1944, Caterpillar was free to design and build its own product lines of bulldozer blades and power control units, pull-scrapers, and rippers. The company started to release its first bulldozing straight blades with cable control units in 1945, and angling blades the following year. Hydraulic blade controls were introduced in early 1947. As for pull-rippers, these made the product line in 1947 as the Cat No. 18 and the No. 28. The first pull-scrapers made the lineup in 1946.

The introduction of the new scraper models really put Caterpillar in head-to-head combat with LeTourneau for scraper market share. The first of the cable-controlled pull-scrapers to be introduced by Caterpillar were the Models No. 60, No. 70, and No. 80, all released in 1946. A smaller Model No. 40 hydraulic-controlled unit made the scene in 1949. A larger Model No. 90 was also eventually released in 1951.

The smallest of these pull-scrapers was the No. 40. The No. 40 was a hydraulically operated unit and was meant for use behind a D4 tractor equipped with the No. 44 hydraulic control option. Capacity of the scraper was 3.6 cubic yards struck and 4.5 heaped. The next size up from the No. 40

Caterpillar's sales leader (15,156 units) among small gas tractors was this Twenty-Two, shown here with a Caterpillar No. 22 Terracer. It was simply a good, reliable tractor. Caterpillar offered a Twenty-Two orchard model, with beautiful, streamlined fenders over the tracks for fending off branches as it crawled through the trees. In production from 1934 to 1939, the wide-gauge version of the Twenty-Two was very similar to the R-2, which had been introduced in 1934.

Author's Collection

was the No. 60, which was rated as a 6 cubic yard struck and 7.5 heaped unit. The No. 60 was designed for use with the D6 tractor. The operations of the scraper were all by cable, controlled from the D6 when equipped with a mechanically powered cable control unit. Up next was the slightly larger No. 70 pull-scraper. This model was designed for use behind the D7 tractor, and like the No. 60, was cable controlled. Capacity for this unit was rated at 8.7 cubic yards struck and 11 heaped.

The Caterpillar No. 80 and No. 90 were the largest cable-operated scrapers in this model series. Both of these units were designed to be matched to the D8 tractor. The No. 80 had a rated payload capacity of 13.5 cubic yards struck and 17.5 heaped. The No. 90 was rated as a 21.2 cubic yard struck and 27 heaped. With 15-inch side-board extensions, capacity was increased to 25.5 cubic yards struck and 31 heaped.

The original rear-end design of the No. 60, 70, and 80 scrapers was considerably altered in later years. The new design featured straddle-mounted, adjustable rear axles that kept the cutting edge level when tire diameters differed. Also, the early units were of a "curved" bottom bowl design. The new units featured a "flat" bottom bowl. These changes also helped raise the capacity of the units.

The updated No. 60 was released in 1952. Its capacity was now rated at 7 cubic yards struck and 9 heaped. The No. 70 was first seen in 1951 with a rating of 10 cubic yards struck and 13 heaped (12 and 15 cubic yards with side-boards, respectively). The No. 80 was the first to be updated. In 1950, its capacity rose to 15 cubic yards struck and 19.5 heaped (18 and 22.5 cubic yards with side-boards). The No. 90 already had the new design when it was first released in 1951.

Starting in the mid-1950s, the pull-scraper model lines would start to go through numerous changes, including being issued new product designations. In 1955, the No. 80 was replaced by the Model No. 463. This was followed in 1956, with the No. 70 becoming the Model No. 435, and the No. 90 now being replaced by the Model No. 491. The No. 40 and the No. 60 would continue on as is.

Introduced in 1933, the gas-powered Caterpillar Twenty-Eight was a very solid performer. It had a four-cylinder, 303 cubic inch displacement Cat engine, with a 4$\frac{7}{16}$-inch bore and a 5$\frac{1}{2}$-inch stroke. The engine had a drawbar-horsepower rating of 30.49 and a belt-horsepower rating of 37.47. Caterpillar sold 1,171 Twenty-Eights by 1935 when production was halted, as customers continued to abandon gasoline for diesel. *Courtesy of Caterpillar Inc. Corporate Archives*

After several previous incarnations, the Caterpillar Thirty (6G) became this R-4 in 1938. The age of gas-powered heavy tractors was almost over, and the R-4 was Caterpillar's final word on the subject. Still, with the help of defense contracts before the final production run came to an end in 1944, Caterpillar sold 4,508 tractors under the R-4 model name. *Courtesy of Caterpillar Inc. Corporate Archives*

Caterpillar started to establish a basis for a self-propelled scraper outfit in late 1940 with its DW10 (1N), rubber-tired, two-axle tractor, with full production beginning in 1941. The original DW10 was powered by a Cat D4600, six-cylinder diesel engine, rated at 90 gross horsepower, though this was increased to 98 horsepower within months of its release. The look of the tractor reflected the truck designs of the time, mainly in the rounded shapes of the front fenders with integrated headlight housings. Because of wartime supply needs, the production of the DW10 was suspended in 1943 and 1944 to create more assembly line space for military production. The DW10 (6V) would again resurface in 1945. It had a bit more power at 100 horsepower, and the sheet metal design of the rounded fenders was simplified, with the headlights now attached by a bracket assembly. Air brakes and rear fenders were also made standard items at this time. In mid-1947, an updated model was introduced with considerable changes. This DW10 (1V) was now powered by the Cat D318, six-cylinder diesel, now rated at 115 horsepower. The front fender and radiator housing assemblies were simplified to lower manufacturing costs. This pretty much eliminated all of the rounded shapes of the earlier models. This design would carry over until early 1954, when the model was removed from the product line and replaced with the larger DW15 tractor.

The DW10 was first marketed by the company pulling the LaPlant-Choate CW-10 Carrymor, the LeTourneau Model LS Carryall scrapers, or the Athey PD10 side-dumping trailer and the Caterpillar designed W10 Wagon bottom-dump hauler. The first scraper attachment designed and built by Caterpillar for its small tractor was the No. 10 (3C), introduced in 1947 for use behind the more powerful DW10 (1V) model series. The No. 10 Scraper was rated at 8.7 cubic yards struck and 11 heaped. In late 1951, a slightly larger No. 15 unit was added with capacity ratings of 10 cubic yards struck and 13 heaped.

For the big jobs, Caterpillar's top-of-the-line, rubber-tired, self-propelled scrapers for the 1950s were its immensely popular DW20 and DW21 model lines. These models—especially the DW21—were really Caterpillar's answer to LeTourneau's big Tournapull scrapers. Both the DW20 and DW21 were designed at the same time and shared most major components, including the engine. The main difference was in the design of the tractors. The DW20 was based on a two-axle, four-wheel layout. The DW21 utilized a tractor with a single axle and two wheels.

Both the DW20 and DW21 Scrapers were first unveiled by Caterpillar at the construction equipment road show, held in Chicago in August 1948. But it would not be until about September 1950 that both models would become available in the marketplace, with 1951 being the first full

When Holt and Best finally merged in 1925 to form the new Caterpillar Tractor Co., the gas-powered Best 30 became the Caterpillar Thirty. Under these two model names, 23,739 tractors were sold between 1921 and 1932, evidence of the reliability and performance of the model. A completely redesigned version, shown here, reemerged in 1935. This one had a four-cylinder, 35.33-drawbar-horsepower gas engine, with a 4¼-inch bore and a 5½-inch stroke. Despite gasoline's qualities, by 1935 it was on the way out as tractor propulsion fuel, and this Thirty could not match the sales numbers of its forebears.
Courtesy of Caterpillar Inc. Corporate Archives

This Caterpillar Diesel Thirty-Five, shown here in 1935, was powered by a three-cylinder, 38.65-drawbar-horsepower Cat D6100 engine displacing 520 cubic inches. It also featured a four-speed transmission. It was only produced in 1933 and 1934, but Caterpillar still managed to sell almost 2,000 of them. At the same time, the Diesel Thirty-Five's gas-powered counterpart sold 1,730.
Author's Collection

year of production. The DW20 (21C for No. 20 Scraper version/6W for W20 Wagon version) was powered by a newly designed Cat D337, Roots supercharged, six-cylinder, diesel engine, rated at 275 gross horsepower and 225 flywheel-horsepower. Its main job was to pull the No. 20 Scraper unit, which carried 15 cubic yards struck and 20 heaped, and the W20 Wagon bottom-dump trailer, rated at 14 cubic yards struck and 22 heaped. Later versions would carry larger 20 cubic yards struck and 30 heaped capacities as the DW20 increased in horsepower.

Early on, annoying design "gremlins" kept popping up with the D337 Diesel Engine that affected the overall reliability of the DW20. Caterpillar was quick to address these problems with the introduction of an upgraded, turbocharged D337F Diesel Engine, with increased power ratings of 300 gross horsepower. The DW20E from 1955 was the first to get the new engine package. With this added power came a revised scraper unit in the form of the No. 456 in mid-1955. This unit was capable of carrying 18 cubic yards struck and 25 heaped. Other models of the tractor included the DW20F in 1958 with 320 gross horsepower, and the DW20G with 345 gross horsepower in 1959. The scraper units used on the DW20G series were the No. 456B, rated at 19.5 cubic yards struck and 27 heaped, and the new No. 482B with 24 cubic yards struck and 34 heaped.

The history of the DW21 model line somewhat mirrored that of its sister machine, the DW20, and what was said of that unit can also be said of this one as well. The DW21 (8W) was introduced at the same time as the DW20 and was powered by the same D337 Diesel Engine. The rear No. 21 Scraper was almost identical to the No. 20 used in conjunction with the DW20; only the design of the scraper's neck and the way it attached to the single-axle tractor was different. Capacities were in line with those of that unit as well. In mid-1955, the DW21 was upgraded into the DW21C model series, as was the scraper unit, now referred to as the No. 470. The DW21C was equipped with the turbocharged D337F diesel, rated at 300 gross horsepower. The No. 470 Scraper was rated the same as the No. 456 unit used on the DW20. In 1958, the DW21D was released with 320 gross horsepower on tap.

And in 1959, the most powerful version of the scraper to be built, the DW21G, was put to work, now attached to an enlarged No. 470B unit. Capacity of the No. 470B was the same as the DW20 model's No. 456B Scraper unit. There was no counterpart to the much larger No. 482B scraper model used with the DW20G, built for the DW21G. In early 1961, the DW21, as well as

In a design departure from the Diesel Thirty-Five, engineers on this gas-powered Caterpillar Thirty-Five decided to cover the sides of the engine compartment with louvered, sheet metal curtains for a cleaner look. Behind the curtain was a four-cylinder, 37-drawbar-horsepower Cat 6000G Gas Engine, with a 4⅞-inch bore and a 6½-inch stroke, displacing 485 cubic inches. Released in 1932, the Thirty-Five was produced for three years, with sales of 1,730 units, and many of its parts were incorporated into the forthcoming Caterpillar R-5.

It is shown here, in a picture taken in 1932, pulling a No. 35 grader.
Author's Collection

A Cat D2 levels the road with a No. 22 pull grader. Added to the Caterpillar product line in 1938, the relatively small D2 (3J/5J) was a performer on the farm as well as the construction site. By this time, gasoline was fading as a source of power for working machines, and the D2 became the diesel-powered successor to the R-2 gas-powered tractor. The R-2 had been introduced four years earlier and had seen three model number incarnations, the 5E, 4J, and 6J series. *Author's Collection*

the DW20 model lines, finally came to an end, but not without establishing Caterpillar as one of the market leaders in the manufacturing of self-propelled scrapers.

A special variation involving the DW20 was the 50C series of four-wheel-drive tractors built mainly as aircraft "tugs" for the United States military. This DW20 model was only built in 1954 and 1955. The civilian variation on this model was the Caterpillar No. 668C Wheel Tractor built in 1956 to early 1957. The No. 668C was a four-wheel drive tractor, powered by a turbocharged Cat D337F Diesel Engine, rated at 300 gross horsepower. The tractor was available with the No. 668S Bulldozer Blade, controlled either by the No. 46 Hydraulic Control, or the No. 27 Cable Control. The unit was also offered in plain tractor form for pulling the No. 456 Scraper.

Other important model lines added to Caterpillar's product offerings in the 1950s were track loaders and pipelayers, which were aimed toward the company's construction customers. Both of these product introductions started as accessory options built for Caterpillar tractors by the Trackson Company, located in Milwaukee, Wisconsin. Established in 1922, Trackson started supplying Caterpillar with pipelaying attachments for various tractors in 1936. In 1937, the company supplied its first "Traxcavator" vertical elevator front loader attachment to Caterpillar for use with the Model Thirty (6G) crawler tractor. Other attachments would eventually follow.

There were 44,307 Cat D4 7U Series tractors built between 1947 and 1959. The 7U version of the D4 had a 60-inch gauge track and drew power from a D315 four-cylinder diesel engine rated at 43 drawbar-horsepower and 48 belt-horsepower. The D4 was big enough for large fieldwork, yet it was well suited to the small- to medium-sized contractor.
Eric C. Orlemann

EARTHMOVER REVOLUTION

By the late 1940s, four models of Trackson tractor loader attachments were offered for Caterpillar equipment. These included the Traxcavator T2 for a Cat D2, the T4 for the D4, the T6 for the D6, and the largest, the T7, which would go on the D7. In 1950, a new design called the HT4 was introduced. The HT4 was meant for use with the D4, but the design of the loader assembly was completely new. The vertical cable-lift loader design was replaced by a completely hydraulic cylinder-controlled unit. The look was completely modern for its day and made the other model designs look archaic by comparison.

Caterpillar liked the Traxcavator tracked tractors so much that in December 1951 the company purchased the Trackson Company outright and made it a subsidiary. By late 1952, the Trackson name was eliminated all together. All of the loaders and pipelayers became part of the official Caterpillar product line.

Models of Traxcavators included the T2 (31C), the T4 (32C), the T6 (33C), the T7 (34C), the HT4 (35C), and the "TracLoader" L2 (36C) and the LW2 (37C wide-gauge). Pipelayer models included the PD4 (38C), the MD6 (39C), the MD7 (40C), the MD8 (41C), and the hydraulically counterweight-controlled MDW8 (42C).

By the end of 1952, the T2, T4, T6, and T7 were history. On the other hand, Caterpillar introduced an all-new model, the No. 6 (10A) Traxcavator Shovel. What made the No. 6 so special was that it was the company's first fully integrated track loader, designed from day one with the loader assembly and tractor built as a single unit. It was also considered to be an industry first. The No. 6 was powered by a Cat D318 Diesel Engine, rated at 76 belt-horsepower. Capacity for the loader was 2 cubic yards heaped. By late 1954, power and capacity had risen to 100 flywheel-horsepower and 2¼ cubic yards heaped.

Keeping the No. 6 company in the revamped tractor-shovel line was the old HT4 and the not-long-for-this-world L2 and LW2, whose end would come in late 1953. The HT4, which was based on the D4 tractor at the time, would remain in frontline duty until 1955, when Caterpillar would wipe the slate clean and introduce all-new Traxcavator track loaders. The smallest, the No. 933C, was introduced in mid-1955, as was the next size up, the No. 955C. The No. 6 Shovel's replacement was the No. 977D, which took center stage as the largest in the group in late 1955. All were new designs that built on the success of the No. 6 machine and would continue into the 1960s in upgraded series with more horsepower and larger-capacity buckets.

This snow-going RD-6 traces its lineage to the Cat Diesel Forty in terms of basic design, but it was given a bigger engine. With its three-cylinder Cat 6600 diesel pulling with 45.38 horsepower at the drawbar, it was a popular performer in the field. Technically speaking, the RD-6 was only produced for three years, from 1935 to 1937, when the tractor was renamed D6.
Author's Collection

This picture of the well-lit Decatur, Illinois, wheeled-tractor line, was taken in October 1956, shortly after the plant was completed. Today the Decatur facility produces motor graders, construction and mining trucks, and wheel tractor-scrapers.
Author's Collection

The forerunner of the D7, and built along the lines of the Cat Diesel Fifty, the RD-7 was originally introduced under the 5E7501 serial number prefix in 1935. Few of these were sold, but with the release, and significant horsepower upgrade, of the 9G model, the RD-7 became a success for both Caterpillar and its customers.

Courtesy of Caterpillar Inc. Corporate Archives

This 1944 World War II Cat D7 tractor is fitted with a LeTourneau Angledozer. Thousands of these tractors were produced, as the government required almost all of the equipment Caterpillar and LeTourneau could produce. The D7 proved to be a handy size. It could fit inside a small landing craft, yet proved it could also handle major dirt moving projects. *Author's Collection*

The D7 tractor traces its roots back to the Cat Diesel Fifty, which was launched in 1933. With small modifications and a bump up in horsepower, it became the RD-7 in 1935, and then the "R" was dropped in 1937. The D7 was capable of delivering 61 horsepower to the blade.
Courtesy of Caterpillar Inc. Corporate Archives

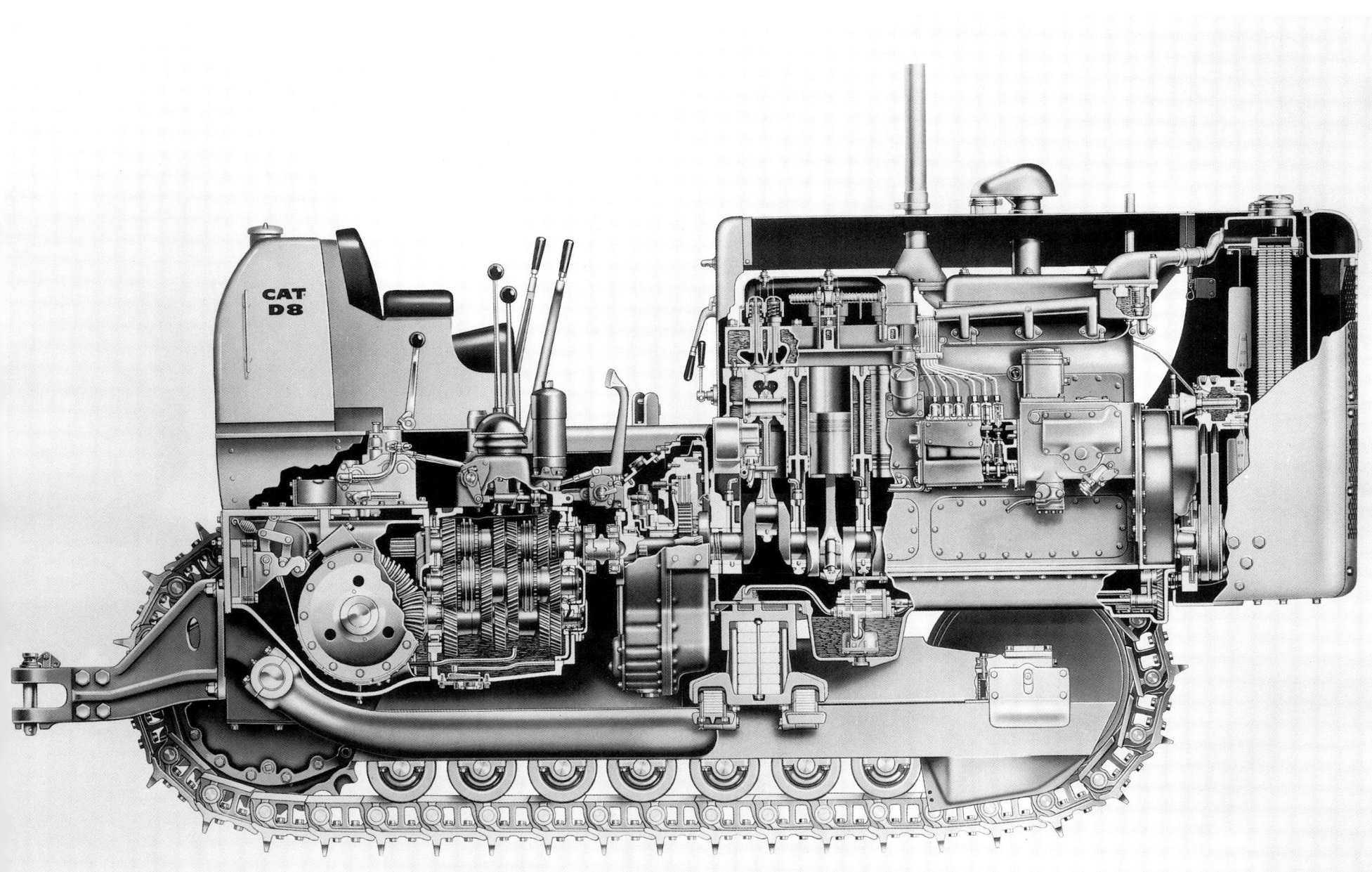

Cutaway of a Caterpillar D8, introduced in 1935, and still in production today as the D8R Series II WHA. Initially designated as the RD-8, the big tractor became the D8 in 1937. The original D8 drew 108.37 belt-horsepower from its Cat D13000 engine to maneuver its 33,110 pounds, had a track gauge of 78 inches and a length of 15 feet, 3 inches. By 1941, belt horsepower had been increased to 131.
Courtesy of Caterpillar Inc. Corporate Archives

The Caterpillar DW10 rolled out in late 1941, claiming its position as the company's first two-axle tractor built for scraper and bottom-dump wagon work. Powered by a Cat D4600, six-cylinder diesel engine initially rated at 90 gross horsepower, this tractor often pulled LaPlant-Choate CW-10 or LeTourneau Model LS Carryall Scrapers. It also found work pulling Atheny PD10 side-dumping trailers and Caterpillar W10 wagon bottom-dump haulers. Shortly after this tractor's introduction, power output grew to 98 gross horsepower. Production was suspended in 1943 and 1944 to make additional space for military production.
Courtesy of Caterpillar Inc. Corporate Archives

In 1944, a sales agreement with R. G. LeTourneau was terminated, which allowed Caterpillar to design its own product lines of bulldozer blades and control units, pull-scrapers and rippers. This put Caterpillar in direct competition with LeTourneau for scraper sales. Prior to the introduction of pull-type scrapers into the lineup in 1946, Caterpillar relied on outside manufacturers for these implements. For instance, the Cat DW10 pictured was a good match for a LeTourneau LS Carryall scraper. *Author's Collection*

The Diesel No. 12 Auto Patrol, introduced in 1938, became one of the most famous motor graders. Part of its success can be attributed to a triple-box-section main frame, which was stronger and more rigid than that of the twin-beam designs found in previous Auto Patrols. But more importantly, the front wheels were able to lean. This shortened the turning radius and counteracted side-draft caused by grading forces. This 12F was introduced in 1965. *Author's Collection*

With the engine mounted high in the rear, the operator had a better view of the blade. The Auto Patrol No. 11 came in both gasoline- and diesel-powered models. The gasoline version was introduced in 1932, while the diesel model made its debut in 1934.
Nick Cedar

Prior to the 1931 introduction of the Auto Patrol, self-propelled graders were referred to as Motor Patrols. These were actually attachments to standard tractors. The rear-engine Auto Patrol with pneumatic tires, introduced in 1931, offered better visibility and greater speed.
Nick Cedar

Above: The No. 11 was produced in both gasoline and diesel versions. This is the gasoline Auto Patrol No. 11. The placement of the engine high and to the rear gave it a cleaner design and increased traction on the drive axle.
Nick Cedar

Left: This Auto Patrol No. 11 used a single rear-axle configuration. No differential was used, simply a large axle. In 1934, a tandem-axle configuration was offered on all of the Auto Patrol models. This helped reduce bouncing and loping that affected single-rear-axle graders. It is now the standard on all current motor graders.
Nick Cedar

The D6 line started in 1937 when the nomenclature of the RD-6 was changed to simply D6. In 1947, Caterpillar introduced the 8U and 9U Series D6 tractors with track gauges of 60 inches and 74 inches, respectively. Power was supplied by a D318 six-cylinder diesel that was initially rated at 65 drawbar-horsepower and 75 belt-horsepower. The tractor pictured is a 1949 D6. The 8U and 9U D6 models were produced until 1959.
Nick Cedar

With cables and pulleys hauling the load up and gravity pulling it down, this T7 Traxcavator could manage just fine without hydraulics. Note the mechanics of the cable system and twin vertical elevator masts that handle the bucket. By the late 1940s, the Trackson Company of Milwaukee, Wisconsin, was making popular loader attachments called "Traxcavators" for D2, D4, D6, and D7 tractors. The Traxcavator lift technology, combined with stout tractors from Caterpillar, proved to be a very successful marriage. Caterpillar eventually purchased Trackson outright, and the T7 Traxcavator entered Caterpillar's official product line as the 34C. *Courtesy of Caterpillar Inc. Corporate Archives*

EARTHMOVER REVOLUTION

A military Caterpillar D8 equipped with a LeTourneau Angledozer, shown here in 1942, is symbolic of the cooperation that existed between the neighboring giants for most of World War II. Caterpillar tractors, combined with LeTourneau blades and attachments built just across the Illinois River in Peoria, enabled Allied forces to build roads and airstrips very rapidly, giving them an important edge over the Axis powers. During that period, both companies went into high production mode to meet the needs of the U.S. armed forces.
Author's Collection

This D8, shown here in 1938, is equipped with a LeTourneau Knockdown Bulldozer Blade. One of many imaginative attachments from the LeTourneau company, this one was especially useful in taking down small vertical structures and trees.
Author's Collection

The first self-propelled motor grader was built in 1919 by the Russell Grader Manufacturing Company and was called the Motor Hi-Way Patrol. Caterpillar initially entered the motor grader business when it purchased the Russell Grader Manufacturing Company in 1928. Pictured is a Caterpillar Auto Patrol No. 11, which was manufactured from 1932 to 1940.
Nick Cedar

This D4 orchard model (4G), shown here without its graceful orchard branch fenders, was a popular model among fruit growers in California. The D4 was born in late 1937 through a simple change in nomenclature. What had been an RD-4 (excepting a slight alteration in the radiator) became a D4. *Eric C. Orlemann*

A Military D4 (5T) with LeTourneau Carryall. The single-tone green uniform of the army masks the competition between these two units' manufacturers, which began in earnest in 1945. An alliance between LeTourneau and Caterpillar had generally left the implement building to LeTourneau, and the tractor building to Caterpillar. With the alliance's official termination in 1944, the two companies went head-to-head building whole machines.
Eric C. Orlemann

Caterpillar crawler tractors, especially the D7 and D8, played an important role in allied operations during World War II. They were used to open up beachheads and build airstrips. This tractor is equipped with a LeTourneau Angledozer and is pulling a rubber-tired LeTourneau Carryall scraper.
Nick Cedar

The 3T series of the D7 was introduced in 1944 and stayed in production through 1955. There were 28,058 units of this version produced. These tractors were powered by the same four-cylinder D8800 Diesel Engine with a 5¾x8-inch bore and stroke that was used in previous D7 tractors. However, the 3T series continued to receive mechanical refinements. A 1948 D7 and 1952 D7 are pictured. *Nick Cedar*

A 1935 Caterpillar RD-8 (1H) tractor with Caterpillar No. 48 elevating grader. The RD-8 was the largest of the "RD" tractors released by Caterpillar in the 1930s, with a six-cylinder, 95-drawbar-horsepower D13000 Cat diesel engine, displacing 1,246 cubic inches. It became the D8 in 1937.
Eric C. Orlemann

In 1963, Caterpillar introduced articulated rubber-tired wheel dozers, close cousins to the company wheel loaders. Today's 854G Wheel Dozer is nimble for a high-production dozer. With an operating weight of 212,232 pounds and an eight-cylinder, 800-flywheel-horsepower Cat 3508B EUI Diesel Engine, it is among the world's largest and most powerful wheel dozers. Its visual similarity to the 992G is no accident; although it uses twin lift cylinders, its platform design is based on the big-wheel loader, and the two machines have the same horsepower rating.

Eric C. Orlemann

CHAPTER 5
HIGHER HORSEPOWER

The D8 was a workhorse for the U.S. military in World War II, with thousands of units finding their way overseas. After the war, the D8 was upgraded to the 2U series. It continued its role as Caterpillar's largest tractor and was continually improved. This 1946 D8 was one of 23,537 2U series tractors produced between 1945 and the end of production in 1953. *Nick Cedar*

Caterpillar first entered the rubber-tired wheel-loader market in 1959, when it released its Model 944A Traxcavator. Even though the term "Traxcavator" was also used for the crawler track-loaders, it also referred to the early rubber-tired loaders as well. The 944 prototype was unveiled by the company in early 1956. Though not a large machine, its standard bucket capacity of two cubic yards put it in competition with a host of similar-sized machines from other construction equipment manufacturers. Its four-wheel-drive drivetrain, rigid frame, and rear steering wheels were design features well accepted in the industry. Caterpillar was looking for the perfect-sized wheel-loader design to get its latest product line off to a good sales start, and the company had found it in the 944A. Powered by a four-cylinder Cat D330 Diesel Engine, rated at 105 flywheel-horsepower or a six-cylinder Continental Model B427 gasoline-powered engine, the 944 utilized a rigid chassis and steered by its rear wheels. At this time, articulated steering for Caterpillar loaders was still a few years down the road.

In 1960, Caterpillar added two more wheel loader models to complement the 944A. These were the 922A and the 966A. The 922A was powered by a Cat D320 Diesel Engine, rated at 80 flywheel-horsepower, with a Continental Model M330 gasoline engine version with the same power output as an alternative. Bucket capacity was rated at 1¼ cubic yards. Its big brother, the 966A, was rated as a 2¾ cubic yard machine. The 966A was powered by a six-cylinder Cat D333 Diesel Engine, rated at 140 flywheel-horsepower. A gasoline engine option was not made available for the larger loader.

All three of these loaders were sized for general contracting work. Big quarry and mining wheel loaders they were not. But Caterpillar was taking a cautious approach to this new market. The limited number of model types fielded in the first few years gave the company time to gain market share and to perfect a new type of loader design that was starting to gain increased atten-

Note the right-hand drive on this 1946 D8 Tractor. These 2U series tractors were produced with slide-bar shifters up to serial number 2U5306. After this they were produced with a conventional stick shift.
Nick Cedar

The D13000 diesel had a 5¾x8-inch bore and stroke and initially produced 95 drawbar-horsepower and 110 belt-horsepower. These ratings increased over time to eventually reach 130 drawbar-horsepower and 148 belt-horsepower. The diesel engine in the 1946 D8 pictured was rated at 113 drawbar-horsepower and 132 belt-horsepower.
Nick Cedar

tion in the industry. This design did not steer by its rear wheels, but by a hinged, or articulated, steering frame. The articulated-steering wheel loader was far more maneuverable than a rigid type and offered superior productivity gains in all working conditions. Though Caterpillar's rigid frame loaders were well received in the industry, these three models would seem antiquated when compared to the new models, the 966B and 988, that the company had up its sleeve.

Both the 988 and 966B Traxcavator articulated-steering wheel loaders were introduced to Caterpillar officials at a special demonstration in February 1962. But it would still be months before either loader would be ready for commercial release. Finally, in January 1963, the 988 was officially sanctioned for sale, followed by the smaller 966B in June of that same year. The 988 was a 300-flywheel-horsepower, 58,500-pound loader, with a bucket payload capacity ranging from 5 to 6½ cubic yards. The 966B came with 150 flywheel-horsepower, a 31,000-pound operating weight, and a bucket range of 2½- to 5 cubic yard capacities. The new 988 was almost twice as large as the 966B. It is also no coincidence that the 988 was introduced within weeks of the newly designed 769 off-highway truck reaching full production status in 1963.

The 769, a 35-ton-capacity truck, was a perfect match for the 988. Caterpillar marketing often promoted the virtues of the articulated 988 in conjunction with the 769. The 769 was in fact Caterpillar's first true off-highway, rear-dump truck. Developed in the late 1950s, the 769 would go through four pilot design stages starting in 1959. By November 1962, the fourth and final pilot truck was the one accepted for production, which would commence in January 1963. The 769 was powered by a Cat D343 Diesel Engine, rated at 375 flywheel-horsepower. Other key features were its use of an independent, pneumatic-oil suspension system, and oil-cooled disc brakes on the rear drive wheels. As mentioned before, its load capacity was set at 35 tons. By 1964, power had been increased to 400 flywheel-horsepower. In late 1966, an upgraded 769B model was introduced featuring a new V-bottom dump-box to reduce rear-end spillage. Also, power was increase to 415 flywheel-horsepower. No matter how you look at it, the 769/769B changed the buying habits of customers the world around concerning a 35-ton off-highway hauler. They would be the first of the company's new mechanical drive hauler product line, that would soon evolve into one of the most popular quarry and mining truck lines in the industry today.

Introduced with the RD-8 (1H series) in 1935, a D13000 six-cylinder diesel powered all of the early D8 Tractors through the 13A series in 1955. It carried Caterpillar through the war years and proved troublefree in thousands of tractors. There are D13000 Diesel Engines that are now over 50 years old still in operation. Some people credit the slow engine speed of 1,000 rpm with the long operating life.
Nick Cedar

During the 1960s, the Caterpillar 988 was kept on a steady diet of improvements and power increases to keep it in step with the marketplace. By 1968, the loader carried a 325-flywheel-horsepower rating and weighed in at 66,000 pounds. Largest bucket specified was a general purpose 6½ cubic yard unit. The 988 was a fairly large machine for its day, but large wheel loaders being produced by competitors were targeted at satisfying the mining industry's appetite for ever larger and more productive equipment. Though the 988 could be found in mining operations the world over, its real sales success was in the quarry and aggregate industries. As the 988 loader model line began to find its feet in the marketplace, Caterpillar engineers began to set their sights on this much larger machine. This loader would be designed to match haul trucks in the 50- to 90-ton payload capacity size class. A large number of trucks in the marketplace were already a perfect match for this new loader. If designed correctly, it would guarantee solid sales for years to come.

Other small-to-midsize wheel loaders introduced by Caterpillar during the 1960s were the Models 922B in 1962, the 950 in 1964, the 980 in 1966, the 930 in 1968, and the 920 in 1969. All of these loaders were an articulated-steering design except the 922B. The 922B and the 944 were the last rigid-frame loaders. They stayed in this configuration until both were discontinued in 1968.

Of all the company's wheel loaders manufactured in the 1960s, the Caterpillar 992 was without a doubt the greatest. Simply put, the 992 was the largest and most powerful wheel loader the company would produce in the 1960s, and would eventually become the best-selling wheel loader in its size class in the world. The loader was first seen in prototype form in late 1965, the first of many 992 machines. At this point the 992X1—as this early design was called—was powered by an eight-cylinder, Cat D346 Diesel Engine, rated at 500 flywheel-horsepower. Capacity of the first pilot machine was 8½ cubic yards. In January 1966, the 992X1 was shipped to Clarkson Construction Company in St. Louis, Missouri, to start its field testing trials.

After months of design evaluations, a second prototype 992X2 was built in December 1966. This unit was powered by a more powerful V-12 Cat D348 Diesel Engine, rated at 550 flywheel-horsepower, the engine of choice when the loader was finally released for sale in 1968. The 992X2 was rated as a 10 cubic yard machine, with a bucket payload capacity of 30,000 pounds. The first production 992 loader went into service at the Duval Mines in Twin Buttes, located south of Tucson, Arizona, around October 1968.

Track loaders such as this one were important new additions to the Caterpillar line in the 1950s and 1960s, expanding the company's reach to a wider construction market. The 951B track loader, shown here, was launched in 1967. It had 85 horsepower, and wielded a 1.5 cubic yard, front-loader bucket.
Author's Collection

This 983 Track Loader fills its 35-ton 769B partner 5 cubic yards at a time. Well matched as an earthmoving team, both of these machines ended production in 1978. The track loader had a working weight of 75,980 pounds and a 275-flywheel-horsepower engine, while the hauler was only 61,800 pounds empty, but had 415 horses pulling the load.
Courtesy of Caterpillar Inc. Corporate Archives

The 992 looked much like the 988, but it was larger all the way around. Its overall operating weight with this bucket attachment was 120,500 pounds—almost twice the weight of the smaller 988. With its Cat D348 Diesel Engine and planetary full-power-shift automatic three-speed transmission, and articulated frame, the 992 proved to be one tough loader out in the field. But this was just the start of the 992 model line's evolution.

In 1973, Caterpillar introduced an updated B-model series of the 992. The 992B contained numerous mechanical changes aimed at increasing the reliability and productivity of the machine. The powerplant and horsepower output were unchanged from the previous 992 model. New for this model was a pin-on ROPS cab, which protected the operator in the event of a roll-over accident, and completely sealed oil-cooled disc-brakes. Though the loader's capacity remained unchanged from the previous model, the operating weight was now up to 135,300 pounds. Again, like its predecessor, the 992B kept raking in the sales.

For the really big mining jobs, one didn't need to look any further than the 992C, which replaced the 992B in late 1977. The 992C was a very muscular mining loader. From any angle, the 992C looked like it meant business. This giant was all about power and productivity. In the rear beat the heart of a V-12 Cat 3412 Diesel Engine, rated at 690 flywheel-horsepower. This extra power came in handy, since the loader's capacity had also risen to 12½ cubic yards. This was also due in part to the redesigned lift arms, which included the use of Z-bar loader linkage design.

A close cousin to the wheel loaders were the articulated rubber-tired wheel dozers that Caterpillar introduced in 1963. The 834 was the largest, followed by the 824. Both wheel dozers were powered by the Cat D343 Diesel Engine. The 834 was rated at 360 flywheel-horsepower, while the 824 had a bit less to play with at 250 flywheel-horsepower. Both models would receive periodic power increases throughout the decade. The 834 was increased to 400 flywheel-horsepower in 1966. The small dozer became the 824B in 1965, with power increased up to 275 flywheel-horsepower, which was followed by another increase in 1969 to 300 flywheel-horsepower. Both the 834 and 824 model lines were available as tamping-foot compactors, when equipped with heavy-duty tamping-foot steel wheels. These compactors became separate model lines starting in 1970, first with the 825B, followed by the 835.

Above: The large DW20 rubber-tired wheel tractor hit the market in 1950. The initial tractors were powered by a newly designed Cat D337 six-cylinder diesel engine that featured a Roots supercharger. Gremlins with this power plant, which affected reliability, were quickly addressed with the introduction of a turbocharged D337F Diesel Engine. The DW20F pictured produced 320 gross horsepower and was capable of moving an 18 cubic yard struck and 25 cubic yard heaped capacity with its No. 456 scraper.
Courtesy of Caterpillar Inc. Corporate Archives

Left: The East Peoria tractor plant, shown here in 1946. Today, East Peoria still produces tractors, as well as pipelayers, undercarriages, and power-shift and countershaft transmissions and gears.
Author's Collection

HIGHER HORSEPOWER

The Cat D9 was launched in 1955, with the first version known as the D9D. It was the largest tractor in the company's line at that time and was offered in two versions, the 18A with a direct-drive transmission and the 19A with a torque converter. It initially drew power from a new D353 six-cylinder, turbocharged diesel engine that was rated at 230 drawbar-horsepower and 286 flywheel-horsepower. One year later these ratings were increased to 260 drawbar-horsepower and 320 flywheel-horsepower.
Nick Cedar

This 1957 Cat 668 four-wheel-drive tractor, a variation of the DW20 Wheel Tractor, is equipped with a No. 668S Bulldozer. Although the No. 668C Wheel Tractor was a civilian variation, the U.S. Navy used the tractor pictured. A Cat D337F Diesel Engine provided 300 gross horsepower. Only 48 units of the No. 668C were ever built. *Author's Collection*

HIGHER HORSEPOWER 187

For big earthmoving projects in the 1950s, Caterpillar offered its top-of-the-line self-propelled DW21 Wheel Tractor-Scraper. The DW21 shared most of its major components with the DW20 Wheel Tractor. The difference was the DW21 was a single-axle tractor and the DW20 was a two-axle design. This 1952 DW21 was capable of moving a 25 cubic yard heaped capacity. Power was supplied by a turbocharged D337F Diesel Engine, which pumped out 320 gross horsepower.
Author's Collection

A rare shot of equipment lined up at Caterpillar's Peoria Proving Ground, East Peoria, Illinois. The Peoria Proving Ground opened in 1947 and today employs a skilled group of Technical Services Division personnel working on a 3,065 acres of heavy clay soils. The clay and extreme winter temperatures provide conditions suitable for a wide range of machine performance testing. Testing methods at the site are meticulous in order to ensure accuracy. After each test, the displaced earth is carefully recompacted in its original position to a specific consistency and density, ready for the next test.
Author's Collection

These 1947 Cat D8 2U series tractors are pulling Cat No. 80 scrapers. The Cat No. 60, No. 70 and No. 80 cable-controlled pull scrapers were all released in 1946 and marked the company's entry into this market. The No. 80 had a rated payload capacity of 13½ cubic yards struck and 17½ cubic yards heaped.
Author's Collection

From 1937 until 1951, the Trackson Company of Milwaukee, Wisconsin, built cable-operated front-loading shovel attachments called "Traxcavators" for Caterpillar tractors—the T2 model Traxcavator was built for the D2, the T4 for the D4, etc. Pictured here is a T4 model Traxcavator attached to a 63-flywheel-horsepower D4.
Author's Collection

Far Right: The 54-horsepower HT4, rolled out in 1950, was a D4 tractor attached to a Trackson Traxcavator loader with an innovation—hydraulic shovel operation. After Trackson was purchased in 1951, the HT4 became a separate Caterpillar model type. This one, in a photo taken in August 1954, holds its 1¼ cubic yard bucket high over its 6-foot-tall D4 tractor.
Author's Collection

One of several important breakthroughs in the development of the 769 Off-Highway Truck was its pneumatic-oil wheel suspension system, a staple of off-road trucks to this day. In the system, compressibility of air was used to dissipate impacts on the frame, thereby dramatically extending frame life. The 769 also introduced oil-cooled disc brakes to Cat's line of rear-dump haulers.
Author's Collection

This 613 Wheel Tractor-Scraper was the smallest in the Caterpillar line when it was released in 1969, but its nimble operation and unrestricted access to finished roads made it a valuable part of any earthmoving team. An operator could whip it around in less than 30 feet and, with 150 flywheel-horsepower behind the elevating blade, quickly fill its 11 cubic yard (heaped) capacity.
Eric C. Orlemann

CHAPTER 6
BIGGER AND BETTER

As major contruction projects stated to rise, contractors were hungry for ever more powerful crawler tractors and other assorted road building equipment to help meet their production deadlines. Caterpillar listed to its customers and dealers, and its answer to these cries was a series of legendary tractors referred to as the D8 and D9.

The D8 actually got its start back in 1935 as part of the "RD" series of tractor releases by Caterpillar. Originally, the RD-8 (5E8001) was actually nothing more than a rebadged Diesel

Seventy-Five with a little more power available. In that same year, a more substantial RD-8 (1H) was released. This model was fitted with the new Cat D13000, six-cylinder, 5¾x8-inch bore and stroke, diesel engine, capable of 110 belt-horsepower. By the end of 1937, the RD-8 was now referred to as the D8. By the time this model of the RD-8/D8 was replaced in 1941 by the 8R-series D8, it was pumping out a healthy 131 belt-horsepower. This model of the big Cat was a great tractor, and its replacement was greater still, with numerous mechanical refinements. In late 1945, this model series would give way to the D8 (2U), which featured even more power at 148 belt horsepower. In 1953, the D8 (13A) made the scene and was available until 1955, in which time the tractor model saw its power ratings soar to 185 flywheel-horsepower (flywheel now used instead of belt-horsepower). In 1955, Caterpillar introduced two all new versions of the D8. The D8D (15A) was equipped with torque converter drive, while the D8E (14A) utilized a direct drive system. Both of these tractors were now featured the Cat D342, six-cylinder, 5¾x8-inch bore and stroke, diesel engine, rated at 191 flywheel-horsepower. In 1956, the D8D became the D8G, and the D8E became the D8F. Though the nomenclature was different, both of the new models continued on with serial number prefixes of their predecessors. Other models of the D8 series included the D8H (36A) with direct drive in 1958, the D8H (35A) with torque converter drive in 1959, and the D8H (46A) with powershift, also in 1959.

The D8 was a great tractor for Caterpillar. But an even larger model built by the company in the 1950s would be the stuff of legend—the mighty D9. Of the early large track-type tractors designed by Caterpillar, the D9 is unique in that it was designed from the ground up and not based on a previous model.

Throughout the 1940s and early 1950s, the D8 was Caterpillar's top crawler tractor offering, both in size and power. That would change in 1955 with the introduction of the legendary D9 model series. The company had been investigating the feasibility of a tractor design model larger than the D8 as far back as 1946, but it was not until 1952 that management approved the construction of two prototype units that would eventually form the basis for the D9 project. In 1954, a further 10 examples of the tractor were built. Referred to as the D9X at this point, these units were very close to the production design that would officially be released in 1955 as the D9D (18A) with direct drive, and D9D (19A) with torque converter drive. The production D9D was powered by a Cat turbocharged D353, six-cylinder, 6¼x8-inch bore and stroke diesel engine, rated at 286 flywheel-horsepower. By 1956, this had risen to 320 flywheel-horsepower. In 1959, three new models of the D9 were introduced. These

The direct-drive Caterpillar D7E was powered by a 160 flywheel-horsepower Cat D339, the D7E made its debut in 1961 with a first-gear rated drawbar pull of 32,500 pounds and speed of up to 1.5 miles per hour. It had a track gauge of 6 feet, 6 inches, stood over 7 feet tall, and was nearly 15 feet long. Subsequent versions of the D7E boosted flywheel horsepower up to 180 and came with power-shift transmissions, before the line was replaced in 1969 by the D7F. *Author's Collection*

Omnipresent in today's construction world, Caterpillar's first wheeled front-end loader—this 944A "Traxcavator"—went on the market in 1959. Obviously much different from earlier Traxcavators, with wheels instead of tracks and twin lift arms instead of a vertical mast, the 944A did share rough bucket dimensions and a great versatile utility. Powered by a 105-flywheel-horsepower Cat D330 (a gas engine with the same horsepower rating was offered as an option), the 944A shipped at 11 tons and had a 2 cubic yard bucket.
Courtesy of Caterpillar Inc. Corporate Archives

were the D9E (49A) with direct drive, the D9E (50A) with torque converter drive, and the D9E (34A) with powershift. Power for all of the D9E variations was listed at 335 flywheel-horsepower. In 1961, the D9E was replaced by the D9G (66A), and was available with 385 flywheel-horsepower. The powershift transmission was now the only drive offered for the D9 model line. Last of the conventional tracked D9 models to be offered was the D9H (90V) from the fall of 1974. The D9H replaced the D9G at the top of the crawler tractor product line. With its 410 flywheel-horsepower, it was the company's most powerful single unit design up until that time. It would remain a viable tractor offering until finally being retired in 1981.

Also during the 1950s and early 1960s, Caterpillar designed and introduced a number of fine motor graders that were made to fill each market niche in the earthmoving industry. Some of these included the No. 12E and the No. 112E in 1959, the No. 112F in 1960, the No. 120 in 1964, and the No. 12F in 1965. Most of these offerings were in the 100- to 115-flywheel-horsepower class. A more significant increase in output could be found in the No. 14B from early 1959. This model was the company's first motor grader to reach 150 flywheel-horsepower. Other models of the No. 14 grader included the C in late 1959, the D in 1961, and the E in 1965. All of these motor graders manufactured by the company were considered highly productive road building tools.

But for the really big jobs, only one model would do—the mighty No. 16. When introduced in early 1963, the No. 16 was the biggest and most powerful blade offered by the company. The No. 16 was nearly twice the size of No. 12 and half as large as the No. 14 series and was powered by the reliable Cat D343 Diesel Engine, rated at 225 horsepower. The moldboard was 14 feet in length, with the option of a 16-foot blade. A Caterpillar first on this unit was the use of hydraulic-mechanical controls for manipulating the blade functions. Before this, all the company's graders had mechanical controls.

Caterpillar entered the rubber-tired wheel loader business when it introduced the Cat 944A Traxcavator in 1959. The term Traxcavator was used to describe early rubber-tired and tracked loaders. In 1960, the 966A was introduced and it became the largest of the early loader designs with a 2¾ cubic yard capacity. Unlike current articulated wheel loaders, these early loaders utilized a rigid frame. They were steered by the rear wheels. The 966A drew power from a Cat D333 Diesel Engine rated at 140 flywheel-horsepower. *Author's Collection*

"Greetings, little buddy." The first field D9D pulls up alongside a Cat D2 during a test. Engineers started with a clean sheet of paper to design the D9D, whose innovations had to wait for the development of an economical manufacturing technology. Initial prototypes were underpowered, but with the addition of a turbocharger, the D9D was launched with 286 flywheel-horsepower, more than enough for its 56,765 pounds.
Courtesy of Caterpillar Inc. Corporate Archives

With its full torque-divider power-shift transmission, the No. 16 was the ideal machine for large highway projects, as well as the perfect solution for cutting and blading haul roads in mining operations. The transmission allowed the operator to select from three speed ranges and three types of drive to match the grader to any kind of working condition. This gave the unit a total of nine forward speed selections. Tandem rear drives gave the grader exceptional traction in the worst conditions. Other key performance features included oil-cooled disc brakes on the rear drive wheels, and a rugged triple-box steel frame design. With such features, the No. 16 was all but unstoppable and proved to be a stellar performer.

Its overall speed, productivity, and reliability were unmatched in the industry. Though there were a few machines on the market that were actually more powerful than the No. 16, none could match its overall performance and balance in the field. Caterpillar kept the No. 16 grader program over the years and supplied it with a steady flow of improvements and upgrades that were constantly sending the competition back to the drawing boards in hopes of finding ways of outdoing the big Cat blade.

In 1973, Caterpillar took the wraps off the newly redesigned 16G Motor Grader. This new model series incorporated numerous design and performance upgrades. Of most importance, the 16G now featured an articulated frame, which pivoted right behind the operator's cab. This layout allowed the operator to choose from three main frame positions: straight, articulated, or crab, depending on the job requirements. The blade controls were now completely hydraulic, making blade positioning faster and more precise. A new 250-flywheel-horsepower, Cat 3406 Diesel Engine now resided in the rear, mated to a single-lever power-shift transmission with eight forward speeds. Also, the 16-foot moldboard had become the standard blade of choice in this model series, with the

Cutaway of the famous Caterpillar D9, one of the largest "low-tracked" tractors Caterpillar ever made. Experimental prototypes were in the field by 1954, and the first production model, the D9D, rolled off the line a year later. Subsequent Models E (1959), G (1961), H (1974), L (1980), and N (1987) have chronicled improvements in power and performance up to today's 410-flywheel-horsepower, 107,000-pound D9R.
Courtesy of Caterpillar Inc. Corporate Archives

Ralph Kress, a legend in the earthmoving industry and designer of the first Haulpak truck, was brought on board at Caterpillar during development of the 769, shown here in October of 1962. It was Caterpillar's first true off-highway truck, designed from a clean sheet of paper. Note the easy lines and large radii on the bends in the sheet metal on this 769 — reflecting the style and tastes of its era. *Author's Collection*

14-foot unit made an option. It was the company's finest and most modern motor grader to date. The earthmoving industry simply loved it.

The earthmoving industry also loved the 600-series wheel tractor-scraper models Caterpillar launched in 1962. Prior to that year, the company was a little slow in getting into some of the more sophisticated scraper designs that were being offered by other manufacturers, especially Euclid. But now the company was making up for it in a big way. No less than seven new models came charging into Cat dealers around the country. These machines were some of the largest, most powerful, and most advanced conventional wheel tractor-scrapers ever built by Caterpillar or just about anyone else at the time.

For two-axle wheel tractor-scraper designs, Caterpillar introduced the 641, 651, and the twin-engine 657. For three-axle machines, new offerings were the 632, 650, 660, and the largest of all the offerings, the 666. The Caterpillar 641 from 1962 was the next size up from the 631B at the time. The 641 was powered by the eight-cylinder Cat D346 Diesel Engine, rated at 450 flywheel-horsepower. Capacity of the scraper unit was 28 cubic yards struck and 38 heaped. In 1963, a 641 "special applications" model was added to the line for use in severe loading conditions. The larger 651 utilized the same engine as found in the 641 and carried the same power output ratings. The 651 could handle 32 cubic yards struck and 44 heaped in its large scraper bowl. As with the 641, the 651 got a boost in power in 1965 to 500 flywheel-horsepower. In 1968, the 651B was released with power increased to 550 flywheel-horsepower.

The top dog in the two-axle Caterpillar lineup was the twin-engine 657. The 657 was the company's first two-axle wheel tractor-scraper model to utilize front and rear engines, which provided drive to all wheels. This design was introduced by Euclid in 1949. What made Euclid's scraper possible was the use of Allison Torqmatic transmissions, which would synchronize the front and rear units. But Caterpillar did not have a fully automatic transmission of its own until the company introduced its powershift transmission with the 600 series. Now a twin-powered wheel tractor-scraper was possible.

The 657 used the same diesel in the front tractor as that found on the 651. The rear scraper unit was powered by a six-cylinder Cat D343A Diesel Engine, rated at 335 flywheel-horsepower. Combined with the front engine, you were looking at 785 flywheel-horsepower. Scraper capacity was the same as the 651 model. In 1965, power was increased to 860 flywheel-horsepower, 500 for

the front engine and 360 for the rear. Then again in 1966, Cat engineers found still more ways to squeeze 400 flywheel-horsepower from the rear powerplant, bringing the output to a sizable 900 flywheel-horsepower. For a "push-pull" type of setup, where both scrapers can hook together for increased loading efficiency, special 657 units were introduced in 1968 with all the necessary equipment factory installed. In 1969, the regular model was upgraded to the 657B series, with an increase in power output to 950 flywheel-horsepower, and the push-pull 657B was also released.

BIGGER AND BETTER

The large Caterpillar No. 16 Motor Grader was the first in the company's line to use hydraulic-mechanical controls for manipulating blade functions. Prior to this, Caterpillar motor graders used mechanical controls. The moldboard on this giant was 14 feet long, with an optional 16-foot-long blade available. A Cat D343 Diesel Engine rated at 225 flywheel-horsepower put power to the ground through a power-shift transmission.
Courtesy of Caterpillar Inc. Corporate Archives

Customers who wanted the high-speed stability of a three-axle wheel tractor-scraper needed look no further than the new 600-series offerings. The Caterpillar 632 utilized the same tractor as that found on the 630B. The engine was also the same diesel D343, rated at 335 flywheel-horsepower. The main difference between the two models was the size of the 632 model's scraper, which could hold 28 cubic yards struck and 38 heaped. In 1963, a 632 SA version was made available. Then in 1964, power for both variations was raised to 360 flywheel-horsepower. But the marketplace seemed to favor the larger three-axle scrapers built by the company. Also in its size class, the two-axle 641 model was the preferred machine to have at the job site.

Caterpillar's big three-axle wheel tractor-scrapers were the 650, 660, and 666. All three of these models shared components with each other in one way or another, especially the 660 and 666. The 650 was powered by the Cat D346 Diesel Engine, rated at 560 gross horsepower and 450 flywheel-horsepower. This engine would also be the standard tractor engine in the 660 and 666 as well. The 650 was capable of handling 32 cubic yards struck and 44 heaped, the same as the two-axle 651 and 657 models.

The Caterpillar 660 and 666 were the largest-capacity earthmoving wheel tractor-scrapers ever factory-produced by the company. Both units were rated at 40 cubic yards struck and 54 heaped. The 660 depended on at least two D9 dozers to help push-load the unit to achieve full loads in a respectable time. The 666 could get by with just one D9 because it utilized two engines, front and rear, like the 657. The scraper's rear engine was also the same unit found in the 657, the D343A, rated at 335 flywheel-horsepower. Total output of the 666 was 785 flywheel-horsepower. In 1963, the tractors on the 650, 660, and 666 were all made the same series. Only the decals on the sides of the tractors were different. In 1964, power was increased to 500 flywheel-horsepower for all three units, and in 1965, the rear-engine output of the 666 was jumped to 360 flywheel-horsepower, making that unit capable of 860 flywheel-horsepower. In 1967, the tractor of the 666 model was replaced by a new unit, while the 650 and 660 retained the previous series.

The No. 16 was the largest motor grader of its day. It was introduced in 1963 for large highway projects and maintaining haul roads in mining operations. In 1973, the No. 16 was replaced by the 16G. It was Caterpillar's first articulated-frame grader, which greatly improved maneuverability. The 16G featured a 16-foot moldboard as standard. The pictured 16G was the first articulated grader to roll off the line.
Caterpillar Inc.

Caterpillar introduced off-highway trucks to its lineup in the 1960s. The predecessors to these dedicated haul trucks were often referred to as rockers, which were trailer bodies combined with one- or two-axle scraper tractors. Athey Products Corp. of Chicago built a large assortment of rear-and bottom-dump trailers for Caterpillar's wheel tractor-scrapers, such as the pictured Cat 631A. These were no substitute for a true, self-contained dump truck.
Author's Collection

Finally in 1969, all three wheel tractor-scrapers became B models. The 650B, 660B, and 666B were all now rated with 550 flywheel-horsepower tractors. The rear engine on the 666B was increased to 400 flywheel-horsepower, increasing total output of that unit to 950 flywheel-horsepower. This would be the last major change in the three-axle lineup. The 650B would officially come to an end in 1972, while the 666B would soldier on until 1978, when it too would stop production. The last of the big three-axle wheel tractor-scrapers built was the 660B. On February 7, 1979, the last 660B tractor rolled off the assembly line at Caterpillar's Decatur plant. After this, the book was closed on three-axle wheel tractor-scraper production at Caterpillar.

After the landslide of wheel tractor-scraper introductions in 1962, Caterpillar would add only a few more new models in the 1960s. One of these was the Model 621, which was introduced in mid-1965 as the replacement for the 619C. The 621 was now completely hydraulic controlled, as opposed to the cable controls on the old 619C unit. The 621 was powered by an eight-cylinder Cat D336 Diesel Engine, rated at 300 flywheel-horsepower. Load capacity for the scraper bowl was just a bit more than the 619C, with ratings of 14 cubic yards struck and 20 heaped.

In 1968, Caterpillar released its very popular, twin-engine 627 model line. This was the third model to utilize two drivetrains, just like the previously released 657 and 666 machines. The 627 was a completely new design and was not based on an upgrade from a prior model. Its engines were the six-cylinder Cat D333T Diesel Engines, both front and rear. Total output was 450 flywheel-horsepower, or 225 flywheel-horsepower from each unit. Capacity rating for the 627 was 14 cubic yards struck and 20 heaped, the same as the Model 621. In 1969, the 627 push-pull model was officially released. Much like a regular 627, it was factory equipped with the necessary front and rear equipment to allow both units to be hooked together for faster loading cycles.

To add a further dimension to its wheel tractor-scraper offerings, Caterpillar introduced the J619 wheel tractor-scraper in 1964. The J619 utilized a hydraulically powered, elevator type of

In 1962 the two-axle 641 with a 28 cubic yard struck capacity and 38 cubic yard heaped capacity was one of seven new 600-series wheel tractor-scrapers, which brought Caterpillar to the leading edge of scraper design. Originally, the 641 relied on an eight-cylinder Cat D346 Diesel Engine rated at 450 flywheel-horsepower. This grew to 500 flywheel-horsepower in 1965. A revised 641 SA model was fielded briefly in 1968 before being upgraded to a B-series in 1969 when output increased to 550 flywheel-horsepower. *Author's Collection*

During the 1960s several large earthmoving jobs required mammoth earthmoving equipment. One solution was the Tandem and Triple 657s. The Tandem 657 consisted of two Cat 657 Wheel Tractor-Scrapers hooked together. A single operator on the lead scraper controlled this four-engine unit. The Triple 657 was basically a Tandem 657 with another scraper added. Because of the 186-foot length, a high-mounted cab was used so the operator could keep track of this 2,850 flywheel-horsepower monster. *Peterson Tractor*

design for the scraper unit built by the Johnson Manufacturing Company. The self-loading ability of this type of unit did not require the help of push-dozers. It would load material in a type of paddle-wheel fashion. Capacity for the model was 20 cubic yards heaped. The tractor front of the J619 was the same as the regular 619C scraper. In mid-1965, the J619 was replaced by the improved J621. The J621 utilized the same tractor as the normal 621. Its Johnson elevating scraper was capable of handling 21½ cubic yards heaped.

In 1966, Caterpillar took a big step up in the capacity of its self-loading elevating scrapers when it released the 633. The 633's tractor was based on the standard 631B unit and was powered by a six-cylinder Cat D343 Diesel Engine, rated at 400 flywheel-horsepower. The 633's scraper utilized a four-speed elevator that was driven by a single hydraulic motor mounted at the top of the elevator mechanism. Capacity for the 633 was 32 cubic yards heaped. The 633 was the ideal machine for short-haul work. As the loading distances increased in length, the weight of the 633 would slow the unit down. At this point, standard wheel tractor-scrapers would be the equipment of choice. Either way, Caterpillar had all the bases covered.

Following in the tire tracks of the largest Caterpillar elevating grader in 1969 was the smallest model offered by the company, the 613. The 613 was sized to operate in tight working conditions. Its size and weight also allowed it to be legally driven on roads, which would benefit the contractor whose job sites were close to each other. The little 613 was powered by an eight-cylinder, Cat 3160 Diesel Engine, rated at 150 flywheel-horsepower. Capacity for its self-loading elevator scraper was 11 cubic yards heaped.

In the late 1950s and early 1960s, manufacturers were designing and building ever-larger scrapers, many with dual-engine configurations. For maximum productivity, push dozers were usually required to load these massive units. For the largest of these wheel tractor-scrapers, it was quite common to find two Cat D9s dedicated to push loading a single unit at a time. It required skilled

The twin-engined Cat 657 Wheel Tractor Scraper rolled out in 1962. It was the first two-axle scraper in the Caterpillar lineup with a front and a rear engine that powered all wheels. This was made possible by the new power-shift transmission. The front diesel produced 450 flywheel-horsepower and the rear engine pumped out an additional 335 flywheel-horsepower, for a total of 785 flywheel-horsepower. It had a 32 cubic yard struck capacity and carried 44 cubic yards heaped. *Author's Collection*

operators to get the two dozers in position and to match the speed of the scraper in a timely manner. But Buster Peterson from the Peterson Tractor Company of San Leandro, California, thought there must be a better, more productive way of push loading these units. Time was always lost in maneuvering two independently operated dozers in behind the scraper. But what if both tractors were hooked together, so their performance capabilities could be better controlled? Enter the Quad-Trac.

Peterson started to experiment with two Cat tractors, hooked together by a ball-and-socket-type hitch in the late 1950s. But this unit still required two operators to control the tractors. A better system would have to be worked out that would eliminate the need of the second operator. During this time, Caterpillar was releasing new, more powerful and larger-capacity wheel tractor-scrapers. To push load them, only the biggest tractors would do, and more often than not, the mighty Cat D9 did the job. For Peterson's Quad-Trac unit, the tractor of choice would have to be the D9G.

Peterson had the first prototype Quad-Trac D9G up and running in 1963. Two D9G units were hooked together by a ball-and-socket hitch arrangement, with both tractors controlled by a single operator from the front unit. Air-over-hydraulic control lines from the lead D9G tractor controlled all the operating functions of the rear unit. The operator's seat on the front tractor was mounted at a 45-degree angle to the right, making the viewing of the rear D9G possible while backing up without craning one's neck. The front tractor utilized a cushioned inside-arm dozer blade for pushing the scrapers. This blade, designed by Peterson and engineer Fred Stevens, was patented in 1972 and later purchased by Caterpillar. With 770 flywheel-horsepower on tap, the Quad-Trac was all but unstoppable.

In the past, the scraper operator would start his cycle by taking a shallow cut, and then increasing the "bite" as he felt the two independent tractors making contact in the rear. The dual D9G unit could apply full power immediately at the beginning of the pushing cycle, allowing the scraper to start off with a full bite, and shortening the amount of time it took to get a full load. After preliminary testing at Guy F. Atkinson's Briones Dam project near Orinda, California, in late 1963 and early 1964, the Quad-Trac D9G was deemed a complete success. This first unit was then sold to S. J. Groves in West Virginia in 1964.

Caterpillar was very impressed with the performance of the Quad-Trac. Starting in late 1964, Cat started to offer the unit in its product line, with Peterson being responsible for fabrication. In

The Caterpillar Triple 657 Wheel Tractor-Scraper was the most powerful Caterpillar-based scraper ever produced. It was the result of an engineering program initiated by Buster Peterson with Caterpillar to meet the needs of large earthmoving projects in California. The scraper had a load capacity of 150 cubic yards, and only the most skilled operators were allowed to take the controls. *Peterson Tractor*

all, Peterson built 10 sets of dual D9Gs between late 1963 and early 1967. Unit numbers 9-9-103 and 9-9-107 were originally purchased by Caterpillar Research, bought back by Peterson, and then resold. An unspecified quantity of do-it-yourself field conversion kits were also produced and sold, but it is believed that these were small in number.

Peterson was granted patents in August 1966 for the "Draft Assembly for Tandem Tractors" and the "Steering Controls for Tandem Tractors." Not long after this, he sold the patent rights to Caterpillar, and in 1968, Cat began selling the unit as the DD9G. Caterpillar also issued new serial number prefix codes for the unit, 90J for the front tractor and 91J for the rear. All of the Peterson fabricated sets utilized D9G (66A) units.

In 1974, Caterpillar released an upgraded DD9H model of the big quad set. The DD9H (97V front/98V rear) incorporated all of the improvements of the regular D9H model, but with two tractors combined, power output was an impressive 820 flywheel-horsepower. This unit stayed in the product line until 1980.

Caterpillar had been very impressed with the overall design execution of the Peterson Quad-Trac conversions, especially Buster Peterson's multiple engine and maneuvering air controls for a single operator. The company also wanted to produce a powerful bulldozer to match what competitors were already offering. Peterson and his design group got the job for the machine that would be an outgrowth of the Quad-Trac D9G. A concept model of the dozer, made out of two toy Cat tractors, was approved to go to the next step—a full-size operating prototype.

By late 1966, the prototype was ready for testing. Unique to this unit was its use of a single hydraulic cylinder, mounted on the front nose of each D9G tractor, to control the movement of its massive blade. Caterpillar liked what it saw, even though further design work would be needed to bring the big dozer up to production standards. In 1967, Cat Research took over the project. By late 1969, a finalized version of the SxS D9G (29N left side/30N right) was officially introduced by Caterpillar. High-volume production dozing was what this brute was all about. With its 24-foot-wide blade, it was an ideal coal stripping dozer. The side-by-side machine also excelled at land reclamation and stockpiling. To push this big blade around, you needed horsepower, and with two D9G tractors combined, you had two Cat D353 Diesel Engines, pumping out 770 flywheel-horsepower at your command. The SxS D9G was connected together by means of a rear tie-bar, a diagonal brace between the two inside track assemblies, and at the front by the bulldozing blade. Operating controls were an air-over-hydraulic system with quick-disconnect lines. The operator controlled both tractors from the left unit. Buster Peterson was awarded a patent on the "Side-by-Side Tractor" concept in May 1972. Like the Quad-Trac designs, Caterpillar would also purchase these patents from him.

When the regular production D9G became the D9H in mid-1974, the same transition occurred with the side-by-side dozer. The SxS D9H (99V left/12U right) produced more power than its predecessor, with 820 flywheel-horsepower now on hand. Most major specifications remained unchanged. The owner also had the option of converting both tractors to single dozer operation if a particular job required it. Production of the SxS D9H dozer finally came to an end in 1977.

The Cat 657 twin-engined wheel tractor-scraper was upgraded to a B-series in 1969. Power was increased to 950 flywheel-horsepower. Later in the year, this wheel tractor-scraper was released in a push-pull version. This allowed the machines to hook together for increased loading efficiency. *Author's Collection*

The three-axle Cat 650 Wheel Tractor-Scraper had a 32 cubic yard struck capacity and a 44 cubic yard heaped capacity, the same as the two-axle 651 and 657 models. The Cat D346 Diesel Engine that powered this scraper was the same engine that powered the 660 and 666 tractors. It originally produced 450 flywheel-horsepower, but this was increased to 500 flywheel-horsepower in 1964. Finally, in 1969 horsepower reached 550 flywheel-horsepower with the introduction of the 650B.

Author's Collection

BIGGER AND BETTER

The 621 Wheel Tractor-Scraper was launched in mid-1965 as a replacement for the 619C. The cable controls that were on the 619C were replaced with full hydraulic controls on the 621. It offered load capacities of 14 cubic yards struck and 20 cubic yards heaped. An eight-cylinder Cat D336 Diesel Engine provided 300 flywheel-horsepower.
Courtesy of Caterpillar Inc. Corporate Archives

In 1969, the three-axle 666 Wheel Tractor-Scraper became a B series. Tractor output was increased to 550 flywheel-horsepower. Coupled with a 400-flywheel-horsepower rear diesel, the wheel tractor-scraper produced 950 flywheel-horsepower. This was the major change to this three-axle machine. The 666B was produced through 1978. The pictured tractor is a 1970 version.
Author's Collection

The Caterpillar 660 four-wheel tractor was primarily designed for scraper applications. But its stability and high power output also made it an ideal tractor for pulling other optional equipment supplied by various allied manufacturing companies, such as Athey. This 660 ready for delivery is paired with a 64 cubic yard heaped, 100-ton capacity bottom dump wagon.
Author's collection

The first production 988 articulated-steering wheel loader rolled off of the line in 1963. The 5 cubic yard loader was powered by a six-cylinder Caterpillar D343 diesel. Initially it was rated at 300 flywheel-horsepower, but this increased to 325 flywheel-horsepower in 1968. At this time, the rock bucket capacity also grew to 6 cubic yards.
Courtesy of Caterpillar Inc. Corporate Archives

This 24-ton D8H Tractor is lifted into the hold of this transport ship at the Brooklyn Docks in New York, New York, and headed overseas. The D8H had a production run that lasted 16 years, from 1958 to 1974, a period that saw a significant increase in the size of Caterpillar's export market.
Courtesy of Caterpillar Inc. Corporate Archives

To control the quality of attachments provided by auxiliary equipment manufacturers, Caterpillar created an approval process to make sure such attachments were up to Caterpillar's standards. Many of these attachments drew power from the front or rear power take off (PTO), such as shown on this Caterpillar D8 2U.
Nick Cedar

Introduced in 1960, the 922A Traxcavator offered a choice of gasoline or diesel power. The diesel engine was a Cat D320 rated at 80 flywheel-horsepower, while the gasoline option was a Continental Model M330 that also produced 80 flywheel-horsepower. This smaller loader offered a rated bucket capacity of 1¼ cubic yards.
Author's Collection

In 1962, Caterpillar introduced the articulated Cat 830M Wheel Tractor-Dozer for military service. This machine was intended for use with three government-purchased pull-scrapers provided by other manufacturers. The original 830M was powered by a six-cylinder diesel engine rated at 335 flywheel-horsepower. This was later upgraded to the 830MB, which produced 357 flywheel-horsepower. This four-wheel drive, articulated tractor was capable of speeds up to 30 miles per hour.
Author's Collection

The D9 earned a reputation for performance and reliability. This may have been partially due to the deliberate product development process, which progressed through several phases. Tractors were monitored through extensive testing at the proving grounds, and 10 D9X models were built and exposed to real site conditions in select locations across the country. It was the largest mass-produced tractor when it was introduced, which pushed the technological envelope.
Nick Cedar

The 666 Wheel Tractor-Scraper, shown here, was first unveiled in 1962 and then upgraded in 1967; these were prime years in the construction of America's Interstate Highway System, and as the largest wheel tractor-scraper in the Cat inventory, the 666 was a major player. With 40,000 miles of divided highway to build, the scraper's 54 cubic yard capacity (heaped) and almost 1,000 gross horsepower were welcome assets.
Eric C. Orlemann

The largest Caterpillar diesel-electric-drive vehicle ever built was the experimental 240-ton-capacity 786 Coal Hauler, unveiled in 1965. It shared many driveline components with the 779 and 783 Off-Highway Trucks and shared a similar fate, as Caterpillar ended work on diesel-electric drives in 1969 and the five prototype 786 Coal Haulers were parked. This behemoth was 96 feet long and weighed in fully loaded at 670,000 pounds. Two tractors were used, and the front axle on each tractor put the power to the ground. Testing of this experimental unit was conducted at Southwestern Illinois Coal's Captain Mine. *Caterpillar Inc.*

BIGGER AND BETTER 231

This 1965 prototype Caterpillar 783 Off-Highway Truck utilized diesel-electric drive and was rated at a 100-ton capacity. It featured a three-axle design, with only the middle axle being driven. A side-dumping body was capable of unloading from the right or left side, at the discretion of the operator. Both the front and the rear axle steered the truck. Field trials questioned a few of the design concepts, and this was the only 783 ever built. *Author's Collection*

The 992 was the largest wheel loader Caterpillar produced in the 1960s. Released for sale in 1968, the 992 was rated as a 10 cubic yard machine with a bucket payload capacity of 30,000 pounds. It drew power from a massive Caterpillar V12 D348 Diesel Engine that pumped out 550 flywheel-horsepower. The overall working weight of the early 992 was 120,500 pounds.
Caterpillar Inc.

The invention of the Quad-Trac tractor arrangement saved valuable time maneuvering independently controlled units into line for a big push. Buster Peterson's brainchild, the Peterson Quad-Trac D9G shown here, allowed one operator to do the job faster and cheaper. With both Caterpillar D9Gs working together, 770 horses were pushing the pile, and no scraper was too large to load. Peterson later sold his patents to this machine, and in 1968 Caterpillar released the Dual D9G. *Peterson Tractor*

This picture reveals the awesome power of combined heavy-duty D9G Tractors as they push load a twin-engined Caterpilar 666 through deep, soft soil.
Author's Collection

BIGGER AND BETTER 237

Strictly speaking, the parasol is not a factory option on this 834 Wheel Dozer, pictured in May 1965. The 834 and the smaller 824 were the first wheel dozers ever made by Caterpillar, both launched in 1963. The articulated 834 was powered by a 360-flywheel-horsepower Cat D343 Diesel Engine, was 25 feet, 5 inches long, and weighed around 90,000 pounds.
Courtesy of Caterpillar Inc. Corporate Archives

A September 1964 shot of the 43-foot-7-inch-long, two-axle 631B Wheel Tractor-Scraper. Capable of gathering 21 cubic yards (struck), 30 cubic yards (heaped) the 631B was a solid midsized scraper when it joined the Caterpillar line in 1962. It was shipped from the factory at 70,200 pounds, with a 360-horsepower engine.
Courtesy of Caterpillar Inc. Corporate Archives

This is a 14D Motor Grader, photographed in September 1962. The 14D was the most powerful motor grader in the fleet when it entered service in 1961, with a 150-flywheel-horsepower Cat D333 Diesel Engine. It left the factory at 30,300 pounds and sported a 20-foot, 2-inch wheelbase, a turning radius of 38 feet, and top speed of 21.2 miles per hour forward, 14.6 in reverse. The last one was made in 1965.
Courtesy of Caterpillar Inc. Corporate Archives

This 955H, with an even 100 flywheel-horsepower and a power-shift transmission, was Caterpillar's midsize track loader offering in the early 1960s. It was 15 feet, 9 inches from its rearmost tread to the tip of its 1¾ cubic yard bucket. After its introduction in 1960, the 955H enjoyed a seven-year production run before being replaced by the 955K in 1966. *Courtesy of Caterpillar Inc. Corporate Archives*

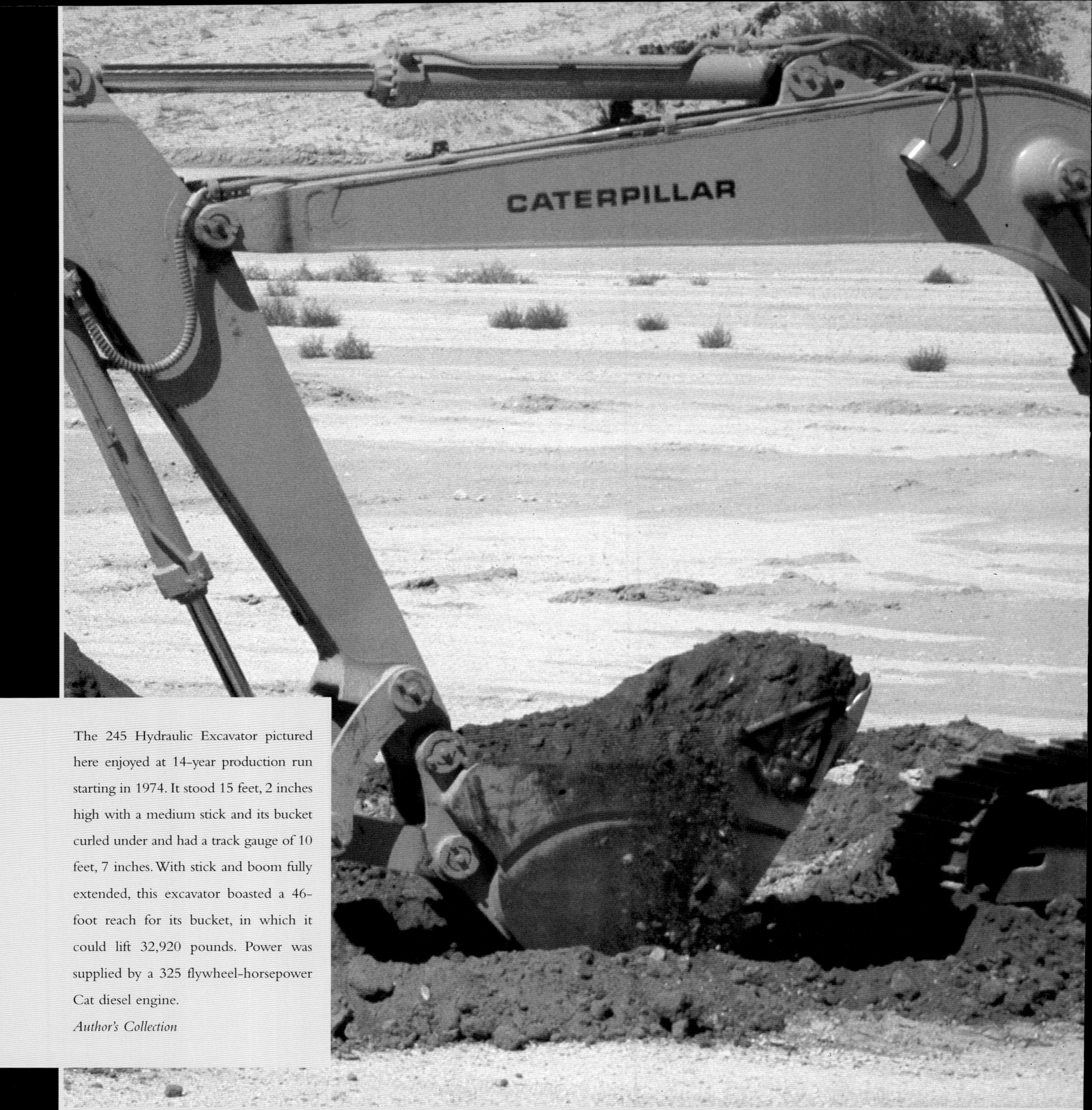

The 245 Hydraulic Excavator pictured here enjoyed at 14-year production run starting in 1974. It stood 15 feet, 2 inches high with a medium stick and its bucket curled under and had a track gauge of 10 feet, 7 inches. With stick and boom fully extended, this excavator boasted a 46-foot reach for its bucket, in which it could lift 32,920 pounds. Power was supplied by a 325 flywheel-horsepower Cat diesel engine.

Author's Collection

CHAPTER 7
DIVERSITY AND DRIVE

Another hardy performer in a long line, the D9H was a worthy successor to the D9G. It enjoyed an eight-year production run, from 1974 to 1981. Shown here with its ripper firmly engaged, this tractor was the most powerful "low" sprocket design Caterpillar ever produced.
Eric C. Orlemann

Caterpillar first teamed up with Mitsubishi Heavy Industries Ltd. in 1962, when the companies formed an equal-ownership manufacturing and marketing company. The company, called Caterpillar Mitsubishi Ltd., served to build and sell Caterpillar products in Japan. Some of these products included tracked dozers and track and wheel loaders. The venture was fully implemented in 1963, and in 1964 the company built its first factory in Sagamihara, which was not far from Tokyo. The first product built in the new plant, a D4 tractor, rolled off the assembly line in the spring of 1965.

Through the years, the partnership was very successful for both companies, and in 1987 the joint venture was expanded to include Caterpillar importing hydraulic excavators built in Japan. When the production of excavators commenced in Japan, Caterpillar Mitsubishi Ltd. became Shin Caterpillar Mitsubishi Ltd.

Also in the early 1960s, Caterpillar engineers started to set their sights on a much larger haul truck intended for use in hard-rock mining applications, since the smaller 769 was basically designed for use in large construction and quarry operations. To help put the project on the right track, Ralph H. Kress, the former manager of truck development for LeTourneau-Westinghouse and designer of the first trend-setting Haulpak truck, was hired in 1962 as manager of truck development for the Research and Engineering Department of the Caterpillar Tractor Co.

After numerous market studies, the company decided to make the hauler a diesel-electric-drive truck with a targeted 75-ton capacity. This hauler would be the 779. The 779 was designed and built along side two other experimental prototype hauler concepts that also utilized the electric-drive system found in the 75-ton truck. These included the 100-ton capacity 783 side-dump, and the massive 240-ton capacity 786 transit coal hauler.

The 779 was powered by a twin-turbocharged and after-cooled V-12 Cat D348, Diesel Engine, rated at 960 flywheel-horsepower. The electric drive system was Cat designed and built, employing an engine-driven traction generator, which supplied direct current to two traction motors mounted in the rear axle, one for each drive wheel. The suspension system was a larger and more advanced pneumatic-oil cylinder system than that found on the 769. And like that truck, the 779 utilized Cat-designed oil-cooled disc brakes, both front and rear.

By mid-1965, the first rear-dump pilot 779 was ready to start prototype testing. It was delivered to the Cleveland Cliffs Iron Company's Republic Mine, near Marquette, Michigan, for a battery of grueling haul tests. By October 1966, the 779 was given the go-ahead to start full production at the plant in Decatur, Illinois.

After a redesign of the frame, the 779 was officially released for sale in July 1967. At this point, the truck was still rated as a 75-ton-capacity hauler, but in 1968, after further upgrades, including a redesigned dump box, payload rating was increased to 85 tons. The last 779 came off the assembly line in May 1969.

The 1960s also saw a flood of new Traxcavator track loaders muscle their way into the product line as well. From smallest to largest, these models included the 933F in 1958; the 933G in 1965; the 941 in 1968; the 951A, which was built in the United Kingdom, in 1964; the 951B in 1967; and the 955H in 1960, which became the 955K in 1966. For larger jobs, Caterpillar offered the 977E Traxcavator. The 977E was introduced in 1958. It was replaced by the 977H in 1960, which was superseded by the 977K in 1966. This model would continue on until 1978, at which time it was upgraded into the 977L.

Second in the revered 992 series of wheel loaders, this 992B reaches full extension to fill a 773 haul truck. This B model was launched in 1973 with significantly upgraded ROPS (Roll Over Protection Structures), but the engine power and transmission remained the same as the highly successful original.
Courtesy of Caterpillar Inc. Corporate Archives

The largest of all of the front-engine track loaders built by Caterpillar was its 983, which was unveiled in 1969. The 983 was powered by the popular Cat D343 Diesel Engine, rated at 275 flywheel-horsepower. Load capacity for the big Traxcavator was 4½ cubic yards. The 983 found great success in the marketplace and was available with a large variety of bucket options to fit specific job requirements. The 983 would make it all the way to late 1978 before being upgraded to a B model status.

Hauling units would also make a good showing for the company, with many important introductions made that would significantly open up new markets for Caterpillar trucks. After the

A 992 finishes off another load. The 992 wheel loader's 550 flywheel-horsepower Cat D348 Diesel Engine could generate 81,360 pounds of breakout force on a load. *Author's Collection*

misstep of the electric-drive hauler program, the company got back on track in early 1970 with the release of the 50-ton-capacity 773. Looking much like its little brother, the 769B (upgraded in late 1966), the 773 packed a 600-flywheel-horsepower engine under the hood and was rated as a 50-ton-capacity hauler.

The 50-ton class of off-highway haulers, like the 35-ton category, was very popular in the earth-moving industry. Large construction and earthmoving contracts, as well as quarries and smaller mining operations, utilized haulers in this size class in tremendous numbers. For the time being,

Caterpillar was going to let the larger mining hauler market be serviced by manufacturers such as KW-Dart, Euclid, Unit Rig, and WABCO. But this was only to be a temporary situation for the company. As the 769 and 773 hauler product lines began to dominate their respective size classes in the industry, Caterpillar set its sights on the next most popular tonnage class—the 85-ton-capacity off-highway hauler.

In 1974, Caterpillar introduced what would be one of its most popular off-highway haulers, the 777. The Cat 777 filled the void in the hauler product line left vacant after the termination of the diesel-electric-drive 779 program. The 777 was powered by an 870-flywheel-horsepower diesel engine, mated to a seven-speed fully automatic transmission. Other niceties included oil-cooled brakes and an all-new ROPS cab. The 777 would also be the first Cat hauler to be released with the squared-off front-end treatment. This design approach has proven so well thought out that it is still the basis for the look of all Cat haulers today.

With its 85-ton capacity and modern design, the 777 quickly achieved what it set out to do—give the customer a superior hauler with unmatched productivity for its size class. In so doing, it became the dominant force in the 85-to-100-ton-capacity hauler class and became an industry standard for years to come.

During the late 1960s, hydraulic excavators were beginning to be taken more seriously by contractors in the marketplace. As these machines increased in size and reliability, they began to permanently replace cable-operated backhoe designs. American manufacturers such as Bucyrus-Erie; Koehring; Insley; and Warner & Swasey all offered hydraulic excavator designs in various sizes. Caterpillar, on the other hand, had nothing to offer, since they didn't build any in the first place. But this was about to change when Caterpillar would introduce its first, fully hydraulic tracked excavator—the 225.

By early 1969, Caterpillar's Research and Design had the first full-scale wooden mockup built for management's approval. From there, the first ¾ cubic yard capacity pilot machine was completed in January 1970. Officially introduced in 1972, the 225 was designed and built by Caterpillar from the ground up and was not a hybrid, joint-effort machine as tried by some manufacturers in the mid-1960s. The 225 was powered by a Cat 3160 Diesel Engine, rated at 125 flywheel-horsepower. Machine travel was by hydrostatic drive. Average capacity range was from 1 to 1⅜ cubic yards, depending on bucket size and material density.

The 779 Rear Dump Truck was the largest two-axle haul truck developed by Caterpillar when the prototype began testing at the Cleveland Cliffs Iron Company's Republic Mine, near Marquette, Michigan. It targeted a 75-ton capacity and was aimed at hard rock mining customers. Ralph R. Kress, the former manager of truck development for LeTourneau Westinghouse, and designer of the first Haulpak truck, led development of this diesel-electric-drive truck. The Cat D348 V-12 diesel engine was rated at 960 flywheel-horsepower and the Cat-designed electric-drive system supplied direct current to two traction motors mounted in the rear axle, one for each drive wheel.

Author's Collection

D9s could be combined as quads (two D9s in line, one ahead of the other) or in a side-by-side arrangement. This pair of Caterpillar SxS D9H Tractors, called the "Double Dude," was produced by Russell & Sons Construction Company and aimed at high-production operations. The unit pictured has a 48-foot wide blade and 820 horsepower, and weighs over 183,000 pounds.
Author's Collection

But the 225 was only the beginning. In 1973, Caterpillar introduced a slightly larger model in the form of the 235. This was followed in 1974 by the rather large 245 series, considered by many to be one of the company's best excavator designs of the 1970s and 1980s. The 235 excavator was powered by a 195-flywheel-horsepower Cat 3306 Diesel Engine. Average capacity was around 1½ cubic yards. The larger 245 machine got its power from a Cat 3406 Diesel Engine, rated at 325 flywheel-horsepower. Bucket payload range was from 2 to 3¼ cubic yards.

The company rounded out its excavator model line with the introduction of the smaller 215, which was built at Caterpillar's assembly plant in Belgium. To further broaden the appeal of its new excavator line, the company offered the quarry and smaller mining industries front shovel versions of the 245 in 1976 and the 235 in 1978. All of these models were well accepted in the industry and helped establish the hydraulic excavator product line as one of the company's most important and profitable for future sales.

In the mid-1960s, Caterpillar began to realize that a crawler tractor larger than the popular D9 series was going to be needed in the not-to-distant future. The quest for a new type of drive system for this larger tractor actually got its start with a Caterpillar research engineer by the name of Bob Purcell. To begin, Purcell was investigating other forms of track drive arrangements that might offer tractive capabilities superior to the designs currently in favor at the time. He found that a triangle-track drive arrangement, or elevated sprocket, in conjunction with an oscillating lower track bogey, seemed to offer the most promise. To test his design theories, he had the Caterpillar model shop fabricate a triangle-track assembly with oscillating bogies. This design was then incorporated into an experimental test tractor built out of odds and ends of a riding lawnmower in 1965.

The simple tractor steered by means of an articulated frame, with a single-track assembly in the front and two wheels on the rear. This experiment demonstrated how the oscillating bogie kept

The 988 Traxcavator, shown here in August of 1969, was the first wheel loader from Caterpillar with an articulated frame—a joint between the front and rear wheels allowing greater freedom of movement. With a shipping weight of 58,530 pounds, a 6½ cubic yard bucket, and a 300-flywheel-horsepower Cat D343 diesel engine, it was by far the biggest at the time of its release in 1963.
Courtesy of Caterpillar Inc. Corporate Archives

the track firmly on the ground when driven by an elevated sprocket drive. Tested at Caterpillar's Peoria Proving Grounds, it performed far beyond anyone's expectations. To prove the viability of the triangle-track's capabilities even further, it was hitched to a Jeep to see how it would handle pulling such a load. The engineers were amazed once again as the little test tractor pulled the Jeep around the proving grounds without breaking traction. The engineers who had witnessed the demonstration knew that they were on to something, but more testing would have to be done to prove to the powers-that-be that this design was the wave of the future.

In 1969, as Caterpillar's research group was tinkering with triangle-track drive loaders, another Caterpillar engineering team was starting to assess possible drive layouts for the D10. Over the months, the two groups of engineers came up with three possible directions for the D10 project. One design utilized a quad-track arrangement with an articulated chassis, while the second was a skid-steer quad-track layout. But the designers ultimately felt that these designs would produce too much ground pressure, and the designs were eventually deemed unworkable. Then the group decided to take the elevated sprocket design of the triangle-track drive and incorporate it into a two-track dozer arrangement. By November 1969, this third concept would proceed to the next level in the design process—a full-size mockup.

A full-size mockup of the D10, built out of wood and cardboard, was constructed to better illustrate the overall size and design characteristics to Caterpillar's upper management. Management liked what it saw and authorized the building of a test-bed tractor. In February 1970, work started on the conversion of a standard D9G dozer, transforming it into an experimental elevated sprocket drive test-mule tractor. This modified D9G utilized an elevated sprocket system with a resilient mounted bogey undercarriage. The resilient undercarriage allowed the track rollers to float over obstacles for an improved ride and better traction. In 1973, after two full years of collecting engineering data from the D9G test mule, the company was ready to begin the fabrication of a full-size D10 prototype in the iron.

Early in the development of the D10 project, there were five primary goals that the tractor would have to meet: high productivity, modular design, simplified maintenance, high operator efficiency, and transportability. The D10 would have to excel in all these areas if it was to succeed in the marketplace. If the customer was unwilling to accept the elevated sprocket system, or if it did not work as promised, many Caterpillar executives' and engineers' careers would be dozed under,

The beginning of Caterpillar's renowned and extensive hydraulic excavator line was the 225 (LC) in full production at the Aurora Assembly Plant by 1972. It had been four years in the making, with a full-size model made of wood built in 1969 just to demonstrate the concept. Driven by a 125-flywheel-horsepower Cat 3160 Diesel Engine and endowed with a lift capacity of 15,600 pounds, it was a very good start.

Courtesy of Caterpillar Inc. Corporate Archives

Above: Following on the heels of the 225 Hydraulic Excavator was the 235, released in 1973 and shown here in July of 1982. The 235 had a full 56 percent more horsepower and was 34,000 pounds heavier, with increased lift capacity and reach. Both models had lengthy production runs, ending the same year, 1986.
Courtesy of Caterpillar Inc. Corporate Archives

Right: A D8N gives the camera a close-up shot of the huge cog-and-steel treads in its high-track shoulder. This elevated track-drive sprocket design, unveiled on the Cat D10 in 1977, removed the tractor's final drives from the wear environment, reduced impact loading, and was easier to service.
Eric C. Orlemann

so to speak. Caterpillar execs were risking millions of dollars in developmental costs, and they were experimenting with the product line that was the backbone of the company's image. A misstep with the track-type tractor line would have far-reaching implications for the company, both financially and psychologically.

On July 13, 1973, the first D10 prototype, identified as the X1, was completed. This prototype featured an open rollover protective structure (ROPS) and two upper track carriers. The following week, it was presented for the first time to company officers and plant managers at their summer corporate meeting, held at the Caterpillar Tech Center in Mossville, Illinois. Needless to say, all were impressed. Six weeks later, the second prototype, D10X2, was ready for testing. The second prototype resembled the first, except it was equipped with a full ROPS cab with air conditioning.

Information gathered after two years of evaluation testing of the first two D10 prototypes was utilized in the construction of the next two test tractors, the D10X3 and X4, in 1975. Though these prototypes resembled the first two units, both featured fully enclosed ROPS cabs and improved resilient undercarriages. The two upper-track carriers on each side had been eliminated. In 1976,

This D10, pictured here in August 1980, demonstrates the acclaimed power of its ripper to break up hard ground. With its 700-horsepower, V-12, turbocharged and aftercooled Cat D348 Diesel Engine, the D10 was the burliest dozer made when it was introduced—and over 50 percent more productive than the D9H. *Courtesy of Caterpillar Inc. Corporate Archives*

during the testing phase of the X3 and X4, Caterpillar started building a new tractor assembly plant in East Peoria. This plant, identified as Building SS, would be the future home of the D10. In late March 1977, the first of 10 pilot D10 dozers came off of a temporary assembly line in the plant while it was still under construction.

With the pilot D10, the company had built its largest dozer. It had also produced the largest, most powerful, and most productive dozer that anyone had built. From this point on, industry and customer perception of what a tracked dozer should be was forever changed. The D10 had a giant blade and rear ripper, along with a V-12 Cat 348 Diesel Engine rated at 700 flywheel-horsepower, and the mammoth dozer was 50 percent more productive than the D9H. The dozer's 10U blade

measured 19 feet, 10 inches across with a 7-foot height, and the large single shank ripper had a maximum ground penetrating depth of 70 inches. Equipped with this blade and ripper arrangement, the D10 weighed in at 191,100 pounds, or 95.5 tons.

Key to the design of the D10 was, of course, its use of the elevated drive sprocket design, which removed the final drives from the work platform and from roller frame alignment shock loads for extended power train life. Its modular design allowed for easy removal and installation of the final drives when servicing was required. Also, the resilient mounted undercarriage, with its four major track bogies per side, allowed the D10 to "ramp" over obstacles. This meant that the rollers and idlers were almost always in contact with the link rails, keeping more track on the ground for improved dozer ride and better traction. Early D10 models were easily spotted by their use of a single, large exhaust stack. But some problems in the engine bay with the turbochargers and the routing of the exhaust system required a redesign incorporating a two-stack design, with relocated air cleaner intakes. This changeover took effect in 1980.

In 1986, Caterpillar released the first of its new N-series of track-type tractors in the form of the D11N. Additional "N" models would join the product line in 1987. The D8L became the D9N; the D9L

Despite its reputation for rugged performance, this modern Caterpillar D10R Track-Type Tractor is actually an efficient, calculating earthmover. With its major components electronically linked and optimized by computer, it wastes no time or fuel on unnecessary motion. Its Vital Information Display System (VIDS) provides the operator with continuous real-time feedback on machine and system operation.

Eric C. Orlemann

became the D10N; and a new D8N was introduced to take the place in the lineup vacated by the D8L. The D11N (74Z) was the replacement for the D10. The new D11N was now powered by a Cat 3508 DITA, twin-turbocharged and aftercooled V-8 diesel engine, rated at 770 flywheel-horsepower. Other improvements included a longer track frame, which placed an additional 21 inches of track on the ground for greater traction and stability, stronger structural assemblies, including the frame, and larger bulldozing blades. Starting in 1987, Caterpillar Custom Products offered a massive hydraulic

impact ripper option for the D11N, which was capable of concentrating 450,000 pounds of impact at the ripper tip, 540 times per minute, to fracture rock. Weight of the tractor equipped with the impact ripper was 225,950 pounnds. In 1993, an updated D11N (4HK) was introduced equipped with an improved Cat 3508 EUI diesel, featuring Electronic Unit Injection. The D11N would remain the top track-type tractor in the company's product line until the introduction of the D11R in 1996.

The mighty D9G, pictured here pulling a 463F Scraper, played a crucial role in the vast road construction projects of the 1960s and 1970s. It had a full 13-year production run from 1961 to 1974. The No. 463F Scraper had a 21 cubic yard struck, 28 cubic yard heaped capacity and was built from 1963 to 1971.
Eric C. Orlemann

Caterpillar dramatically increased the capacity of its self-loading wheel tractor-scrapers with the introduction of the 633. It offered a heaped capacity of 32 cubic yards. This machine proved ideal for short haul distances. The increased weight and rolling resistance would slow the scraper as haul distances increased. This tractor was powered by a six-cylinder Cat D343 Diesel Engine, rated at 400 flywheel-horsepower. The four-speed elevator was driven by a single hydraulic motor.
Author's Collection

This 555-flywheel-horsepower 627F Wheel Tractor-Scraper is tandem-powered, with 330 horsepower supplied to the tractor and 225 horsepower supplied to the rear blade via, respectively, a Cat 3406C and a Cat 3306. Like the 992 series wheel loaders, the 627 series was introduced in 1968 (a very good year) and has earned wide-ranging popularity at job sites.
Caterpillar Inc.

DIVERSITY AND DRIVE

The chassis and drivetrain of this 776 Off-Highway Tractor was based on design concepts taken from the 777 Off-Highway Truck. The machine measured 26 feet, 5 inches in length, stood 11 feet, 2 inches tall, and took 88 feet to completely turn around. Its 109,000-pound shipping weight rested on 27.00x49-36 PR tires.
Author's Collection

With an 870-horsepower diesel in its engine compartment, the 776 Off-Highway Tractor was introduced in 1976. Its success led a number of fabricators to build rear- and bottom-dump trailers for the 776. This one is hitched to a 150-ton Atlas RD150 "rocker" rear-dump trailer. The last 776 rolled off the assembly line in 1984.
Author's Collection

Twin turbochargers and air-to-air aftercooling allow the Caterpillar 3412E Diesel Engine to supply the D10R with an impressive 580 flywheel-horsepower at 1,800 rpm. This 144,200-pound production dozer can be fit with either a 17-foot, 3-inch-wide universal blade or a 15-foot, 11-inch-wide semi-U blade. Automatic control functions on the blade and ripper controls reduce operator fatigue and increase performance. *Nick Cedar*

A D10 Tractor, tidying up the pile for its teammates below, displays its elevated track-drive sprocket just above the shadow in the foreground. This prominent feature created a stir when it was incorporated in Cat's high-production D10 in 1977. Evidence of its success can be seen in Cat's subsequent crawler tractor models.
Author's Collection

Resembling an articulated-wheel loader, the 834B Wheel Dozer has been a steady performer since its rollout in 1974. With a 450-horsepower Cat diesel engine driving its 4-foot, 2-inch-wide tires up to speeds of 21.2 miles per hour (25.9 in reverse), the 834B gives contractors a fast, powerful earthmover.

Caterpillar Inc.

This 772 Off-Highway Tractor hitched to a bottom-dump trailer was added to the Caterpillar truck line in 1971. It had a 600-flywheel-horsepower engine and weighed 70,800 pounds all by itself, but had a capacity to haul 100 tons. It was replaced by the 772B in 1978.

Courtesy of Caterpillar Inc. Corporate Archives

The famous 992 series of Caterpillar wheel loaders began in 1968 at the Aurora Assembly Plant outside Chicago, Illinois. With a working weight of 120,500 pounds, the 992 could carry 30,000 pounds of dirt and rock in its 10 cubic yard bucket.
Author's Collection

The 637 Wheel Tractor-Scraper immediately became a workhorse for the earthmoving industry when it was introduced in 1970. When configured as a coal scraper, as shown, its capacity was 38.2 cubic yards struck and 45.6 cubic yards heaped. In 1975, it left production to make way for the larger, more powerful 637D.
Author's Collection

DIVERSITY AND DRIVE

Easily one of the most successful large crawler tractors ever made, the D11N retains a familiar presence in global mining despite the end of its production run in 1996. Fitted with a 21-foot-wide 11U bulldozer blade rated at 45 cubic yards, this giant can move a lot of earth. An eight-cylinder, 770-flywheel-horsepower Cat 3508 diesel powers the 214,847-pound D11N—and its load—around the world's mines.
Eric C. Orlemann

An original, 1974-vintage 777 Off-Highway Truck waits under the bucket of a 992B Wheel Loader. This first 777, an immediate success in the bread-and-butter 85-ton-hauler class, was the start of big things for Caterpillar, which had been a late entry into the haul-truck business. Subsequent models up to the current 777D have all been dominant, coveted machines.
Courtesy of Caterpillar Inc. Corporate Archives

Small but agile, this D25C Articulated Truck had a turning radius of 52 feet, 11 inches, and measured just under 10 feet wide and 29 feet long when it was introduced in 1985.

It shipped at just over 42,000 pounds, and its 260 flywheel-horsepower engine could manage a payload of 25 tons. *Author's Collection*

CHAPTER 8
GIANTS OF THE INDUSTRY

As the production of hydraulic excavators increased in the mid-1980s, the machines began being teamed up more and more with a type of hauler known as an articulated truck. The combination of the two had replaced, in many instances, the need for self-propelled scrapers in certain working conditions. The articulated haul trucks went where other types of earthmoving equipment feared to tread. With their articulated steering chassis and all wheel drive, they were practically unstoppable, especially on wet and muddy worksites.

Caterpillar first offered a type of articulated hauler, based on one of its two- or four-wheel tractors attached to an Athey "rocker" rear-dump unit, in the 1950s and 1960s. But on steep grades, the performance of these haulers fell off dramatically because of the lack of all-wheel drive. Only the tractors wheels were powered. Caterpillar entered the modern articulated haul truck market in a roundabout way when it agreed to provide complete drivetrains to an English company, DJB

Engineering Ltd. Formed in August 1973, DJB Engineering Ltd. was founded by David John Bowes Brown in Peterlee, England, for the sole purpose of building articulated trucks. From the beginning, DJB haulers would incorporate Cat drivetrains, including engines, transmissions, and axles. In November 1974, the first DJB truck, the 27.5-ton-capacity D250, was unveiled. The DJB D250 was powered by a 235 flywheel-horsepower Cat 3306T Diesel Engine. Interest in the new truck was high, and orders started to pour into the company. The demand would be so great, in fact, that by September 1975, DJB Engineering would have to move to larger facilities to keep up.

By June of 1976, a larger second model called the D300 was introduced, which was rated with a 33-ton payload. Even though these early trucks were designed by DJB, the soul of the trucks, their drivetrains, were Caterpillar iron through and through. Many Cat dealers carried the DJB line, since the drive components were fully warranted by Caterpillar. By the end of 1978, more than 30 percent of all DJB trucks being built were coming to North America. In 1985, Caterpillar acquired the rights and designs for all of the articulated trucks built by DJB Engineering, though the haulers would still be manufactured under contract in the United Kingdom. It was at this time that the DJB company name was dropped and changed to Artix Ltd. Finally, in early 1996, Caterpillar bought the manufacturing company, now referred to as Brown Group Holdings, which included all of the facilities and property in Peterlee. This deal now made everything involved with the production and building of articulated trucks 100 percent Caterpillar.

Numerous models and variations of these articulated haulers have been built over the years. These included two-axle, two-wheel drive; two-axle, four-wheel drive; three-axle, four-wheel drive; and three-axle, six-wheel drive models. Some of the key model introductions included the two-axle D20D in 1992, the D22 and D25 in 1979, the D30C in 1985, the D35 in 1981, and the D40D in 1988. Three-axle versions included the D275, D330, and D350, all in 1978, and the D300B and D400, both in 1985. The largest models built were the two-axle DJB D44 in 1980, and the three-axle DJB D550 in 1978. The 44-ton-capacity D44 utilized a four-wheel-drive system. But for the 55-ton-payload D550, its six wheels were powered on the first two axles only, with the rear axle being unpowered. In 1986, both models were upgraded into the D44B and D550B. In the case of the D550B, all six wheels were now driven, instead of only four. But the market for articulated trucks in this size range was not developing the way Caterpillar had hoped it would. By the end of 1987, both models were quietly removed from the product line.

The year 1985 saw the introduction of the D400 Articulated Truck, a favorite among many contractors as a complement for the Cat 245 Hydraulic Excavator. It featured a six-wheel-drive design, with a 385 flywheel-horsepower Cat 3406 turning the driveshaft. It had a 40-ton capacity, and a convenient turning radius of 52 feet, 9 inches.
Caterpillar Inc.

The Challenger® 65 caused a sensation when it was introduced in 1986 with its Mobil-Trac system, which optimized agricultural tractor performance on tracks. Its rubber tracks paired the mobility of wheels with the tractive and flotation advantages of steel tracks and overcame the steel-track tractor's restrictions on country roads.
Author's Collection

The birth of the Challenger models stemmed from Caterpillar's vision to build a rubber-tracked agricultural tractor. Caterpillar had initially expressed interest in building an agricultural tractor in the 1970s. This design was based on a all-wheel-drive, rubber-tired, articulated chassis design. Referred to as the Cat 4x4 Ag Tractor, X-1, it would start testing in 1979. In 1980, a second prototype, X-2 was also put to the test. At the same time within the company, another parallel program was underway to investige the merits of rubber tracks over tires for agricultural use. Starting in late 1979, a series of experimental tractors were produced to test various drivetrains and track arrangements. After a review by company management, it was decided to merge all of the different research groups together in regard to a future ag tractor, and concentrate on the single goal of building a rubber-tracked ag tractor.

After preliminary testing of the rubber-track concept on a pair of highly modified D6D SA tractors in 1983, engineering moved on to the production of the first prototype Challenger machines. The first two prototypes to be referred to as Challengers were built in 1984. By late 1985, preproduction Challenger tractors were being field tested all over the United States, with a heavy concentration of machines being evaluated on the West Coast. Now referred to as the Challenger 65, the model would officially be introduced by Caterpillar in late 1986, with full production commencing in 1987. The Challenger 65 was the industry's first full production, large farming tractor to be totally designed around a rubber-belted track undercarriage, referred to by Cat as the Mobil-Trac System (MTS).

In late 1990, Caterpillar introduced an upgraded model of the original Challenger in the form of the 65B, as well as an entirely new one, the 75. Both of these models were once again upgraded in late 1992. The Challenger 65C and the 75C were almost identical to their predecessors, except for the design of the front wheels on the Mobil-Trac System. Gone were the tires mounted on steel rims. In their place were steel wheels, wrapped with grooved rubber belts. In 1993, the 70C and 85C also joined the Challenger line up.

In 1994, the company introduced the first of the new "D" series Challengers in the form of the 65D. These were then followed in 1996 by the 75D and 85D. The 70C model did not make it to the D series, with its last year of production ending in 1995. The D-series Challengers were much like their predecessors, except that they had a front-end lighting system mounted across the top of the radiator and more power all around.

Caterpillar surprised everyone again with the release of all-new models in the fall of 1997. The new "E" series marked the first time in the life of the model line in which major changes were made to the appearance of the Challengers. These new designs, with their rounded edges and curves, were extremely modern and up-to-date in terms of styling. The new series included the 65E, the 75E, the 85E, and a new 95E model line. All these models shared the same basic chassis design but differed in the drivetrains with which they were equipped.

It is not surprising that the concept of a highly mobile tractor like the Challenger would somehow find a way to serve its country. The military had taken a keen interest in the Caterpillar's Mobil-Trac System, but it would take some years before a tractor unit would become fully operational in

The 966G is a versatile wheel loader with a wide variety of available attachments, including general purpose buckets, material handling buckets, ground engaging tools and heavy-duty rock buckets. Bucket capacities range from 4.5 to 5.5 cubic yards.
Nick Cedar

the armed services. Caterpillar first tried to interest the military in a Challenger type of tractor in 1986. Caterpillar asked army engineers what they would like to see in future crawler tractor designs. The majority of the suggestions revolved around increase mobility without losing any dozing ability. The tractor would also have to be air transportable on a C-130. Based on these and other comments, Caterpillar initiated an internally funded design program in early 1987 to make such a tractor a reality. In 1988, this experimental unit was introduced as the Caterpillar 30/30 Engineer Support Tractor.

The 30/30 Engineer Support Tractor was designed strictly for military use. The nomenclature of the 30/30 referred to the original performance and design criteria originally targeted by the engineers, 30 miles per hour/30,000 pounds. Even though it employed the Mobil-Trac System, the system was reconfigured for the types of terrain a vehicle of this sort would encounter. The rear drive wheels for the MTS were mounted high off the ground to keep them from being buried in mud and debris. This configuration would also increase the drive system's longevity.

The 30/30 made the rounds to various military bases around the United States and was tested by the French and British armies, but because of budget cutbacks, Caterpillar never received a firm order for any production units.

In April 1996, working directly with the Tank-Automotive and Armaments Command (TACOM) of the U.S. government, Caterpillar once again introduced two revised preproduction MTS tractors, known as the DEployable Universal Combat Earthmover, but officially referred to as the DEUCE. The DEUCE program officially got its start in 1993 as an army program with the U.S. Army Engineer School. The school started working with TACOM in ways to field the DEUCE tractor quickly. Several manufacturers expressed interest in the program, but in the end Caterpillar got the go-ahead for its design in 1995, which was based heavily on the 30/30 experimental unit.

The Caterpillar DEUCE looked much like the original 30/30, but it was a bit "meaner" looking. The DEUCE was powered by a Cat 3126 Diesel Engine. As with the 30/30, two power modes are available: 265 flywheel-horsepower for the "self-deployable" setting and 185 flywheel-horsepower for "earthmoving." The tractor could also be air transported and dropped from a C-130. After successful testing of the two preproduction units, Caterpillar was awarded a production contract for the DEUCE in August 1996 for deliveries to commence in 1997. The first production DEUCEs began rolling off the production line at Cat's Paving Products Inc. plant located in Minneapolis,

Minnesota, on September 9, 1997. One additional unit was also shipped for evaluation by the Canadian army at that time.

Production ended in December 2002. Ultimately, 227 units were delivered to the U.S. Army. In addition, fifteen 30/30s were delivered to the U.K. Ministry of Defence (MoD).

The 980G Wheel Loader is designed to excel in truck or hopper loading, hard-bank digging and general utility work. The pictured loader is screening material to yield a uniform size aggregate. Weighing in at about 66,576 pounds, the 980G handles bucket sizes ranging from 5.0 to 7.5 cubic yards. A Caterpillar 3406E six-cylinder diesel engine with electronic unit injectors powers the Series II Model, pumping out 311 flywheel-horsepower. This engine is mated to a free-wheel stator torque converter to reduce fuel cost per ton of material moved. An integrated braking system reduces axle temperatures and improves transmission neutralizer smoothness.

Nick Cedar

With customers still raising their eyebrows at elevated track drive, Caterpillar complemented this high-sprocket D9L with a low-sprocket design when it was introduced in 1980. But high-sprocket tracked tractors were here to stay. This is an August 1980 shot of a 114,656-pound D9L. With its 460-drawbar-horsepower, V-12 Cat 3412 Diesel Engine with 30-percent torque rise, it could do 7.7 miles per hour in third gear. *Caterpillar Inc.*

When it was released in 1982, the 973 Track Loader was the largest hydrostatic-drive track loader in the Caterpillar lineup. Nineteen years of continuous production followed before it was replaced by the 973C in 2000. It had a 210-flywheel-horsepower engine and a 4.2 cubic yard bucket, numbers that remain unchanged in the new model.
Caterpillar Inc.

The early 1970s were halcyon days for Caterpillar's excavator engineers with the introduction of three great hydraulic machines in three years: the 225 in 1972, the 235 in 1973, and the 245 in 1974. This FS (Front Shovel) version of the 245 appeared in 1976 weighing over 73 tons, with a 4 cubic yard, bottom-dump bucket.

Courtesy of Caterpillar Inc. Corporate Archives

GIANTS OF THE INDUSTRY

A descendant of the venerable Traxcavator, this 983B Track Loader made its construction site debut in 1978. It had a 275-flywheel-horsepower Caterpillar diesel engine and a working weight of 78,530 pounds. A compact machine, just 12 feet 1 inch to the top of the stack and 9 feet 6 inches wide, it still carries a 5 cubic yard bucket.

Urs Peyer

The 992C, with its 12-cylinder engine, had a breakout force of 146,030 pounds and was capable of dropping 12½ cubic yards of dirt over a truck bed 13 feet, 8 inches high. This machine was 14 feet, 11 inches over its tires and could reach a top speed of 14.5 miles per hour in reverse.
Author's Collection

The launch of the now-legendary D10 in 1977 caused commotion throughout the earthmoving industry. It was the most powerful production dozer in the world—but it was the radically new triangular track shape that got everybody talking. In the following years, the bold design proved itself beyond any doubt. Today, all but Cat's smallest dozers feature elevated sprocket tracks.
Eric C. Orlemann

This ingenious 992G Wheel Loader cleans the floor of a quarry nicely with its 16 cubic yard bucket, designed to fill a 100-ton truck neatly in four passes. With a Cat 3508B EUI Diesel Engine delivering 800 flywheel-horsepower, the 992G can develop breakout forces of 137,000 pounds. Its articulating body weighs just over 100 tons and can reach speeds of 12.6 miles per hour forward, 13.9 miles per hour in reverse.

Urs Peyer

CHAPTER 9
NEW GENERATION

A 793B with dump bed raised to its full 55-degree, 43-foot, 4-inch maximum height. A replacement for the bold, 240-ton 793, the B model was introduced in 1992 with an updated 3516 EUI Diesel Engine and a new power shift transmission. By 1996, Cat had sold over 550 of the two models, a very large number for trucks of that size (over 800,000 pounds working weight).
Eric C. Orlemann

In the late 1980s, Caterpillar started development of a large wheel loader that was almost twice as large as the then-current 992C model. The new design, called the 994, was primarily targeted for the large mining sector. In 1989, production started on the first prototype of the 994 Wheel Loader at Caterpillar's newly formed mining vehicle center (MVC), located within the Decatur assembly plant. By September 1990, this prototype finally had its veil of secrecy lifted as the completed loader was dedicated at the plant before being shipped to its new home at a copper mine in Arizona.

The 994 was the largest wheel loader the company had ever built. It was equipped with a standard bucket rated at 23 cubic yards. The loader also utilized a mechanical drive layout. Power for this monster was supplied by the Cat 3516 EUI Diesel Engine, the same engine also found in the 789 and 793 series of mining haulers. Output in this application was set at 1,250 flywheel-horsepower.

The 994 could perform a variety of digging assignments, becoming a jack-of-all-trades at a mining site. It could load 150-ton haulers in four passes, 190-ton units in five to six passes, and 240-ton trucks with seven or eight passes when equipped with the high-lift loader arm arrangement. The 994 also could serve as a backup for a mine's large electric cable shovel fleet. If a shovel was down for repairs, the loader could be brought in to take up the production slack. Once the shovel is fixed, the loader can quickly travel to another work site within the mine. The 994 loader's mobility was one of its strongest selling points. But its large standard 23 cubic yard, 70,000-pound capacity bucket didn't hurt either.

If anything hurt the big Cat during its early months of operation, it was the tires originally specified for the unit. The original 49.5-57 L-4 series tires were just barely adequate for a wheel loader of the 994's size and performance capabilities. But at the time, tire manufacturers no other choices offered. Clearly, something else was needed. Soon, tire manufacturers released a larger design, the 53.5/85-57, built only for wheel-loader use. The tire made an immediate difference in the performance and productivity of the loader. During the first few years, other upgrades were introduced to improve the 994's performance and reliability, such as even larger 55/80 R57 radial tires, beefed up front axle mountings and lift arm assemblies, improved cooling capabilities, and greater bucket options.

In December 1998, Caterpillar introduced an upgraded model of its massive loader in the form of the 994D. From the outside, little was changed on the loader. But internally, significant changes had taken place. The new model was now equipped with the improved 3516B EUI Diesel Engine. New for the operator was the revamping of the steering controls for the loader. The steering wheel was now replaced by a joystick control, mounted to the left of the operator's seat, called the Cat steering and transmission integrated control system (STIC). Because of all these upgrades, the 994D outweighed its predecessor by more than a few pounds. This version now tipped the scale at 421,600 pounds, almost 211 tons.

To date, the 994 series has been by far the best-selling large wheel loader in the world. In fact, more than 200 of the original models sold before being replaced by the D series. Like Caterpillar's successful mining haulers, 994 Wheel Loaders can now be found working in all types of digging applications throughout the world.

The next class of mining haulers above Caterpillar's 789 series is the 240-ton-capacity trucks. The 240-ton class was dominated in the marketplace by giant diesel-electric-drive haulers. Companies such as Dresser (now Komatsu), Unit Rig, and Wiseda (now Liebherr) all had models in this class by the late 1980s. Though many in the industry thought that a power-shift transmission could not be built for a 240-ton hauler, Caterpillar engineers proved them wrong with the 793.

The new 240-ton Caterpillar 793 hauler was simply the world's largest mechanical-drive truck when it started to roll out of Decatur assembly plant in January 1991. No one thought a truck of this size could be reliably equipped with a mechanical automatic transmission and rear differential. No one, that is, but Cat. The new six-speed transmission was mated to the tried-and-true Cat 3516 Diesel Engine. But as installed in the 793, a higher power output was dialed in, producing a healthy 2,057 flywheel-horsepower.

Overall, the 793 was a smart-looking truck. It was also the company's first hauler to mount the front access ladder in front of the radiator, making it less steep and safer for the operator and maintenance crews. The first few fleets of the 793 were followed very closely by Cat engineers. The company had its reputation on the line with these trucks in the mining industry, and the competition would surely bring any perceived fault to the attention of prospective customers.

The 793 performed well in the field, but not without the typical growing pains usually encountered in a totally new design. These were quickly addressed in the autumn of 1992 with the introduction of the 793B series. The big hauler received the updated 3516 EUI Diesel Engine, the same as that found in the 785B and 789B. The 793B also was installed with a second-generation, electronically controlled, six-speed power-shift transmission, which addressed some of the weaknesses that had surfaced during the early months of the 793 program introduction. The new unit offered improved powertrain service life, smoother shifting, and electronic control of driveline torque during forward and reverse shifts. After

This was the first modern 994 Wheel Loader to roll of the assembly line in 1990, though the first experimental version of it was built in 1969. The earlier 994 has virtually nothing in common with the modern version. With a 20 cubic yard bucket capacity, this giant, one-of-a-kind loader was a diesel-electric-drive design powered by a 960-flywheel-horsepower V-12 diesel engine.
Caterpillar Inc.

these upgrades, the big hauler really started to hit its stride in the marketplace. By mid-1996, more than 550 units of the 793 and 793B haulers had been placed into service at mining locations throughout the world.

The company kept the pressure on its competition by releasing a more powerful model of the big hauler in mid-1996, in the form of the 793C. As with its smaller brothers, the 793C received the improved Cat 3516B EUI Diesel Engine, with the appropriate increase in power— 2,166 flywheel-horsepower now on tap. Capacity remained unchanged at 240 tons. Other improvements included redesigned hydraulic systems, more robust transmission clutch plates and discs, and enhanced diagnostic electronics.

The first of the new generation of Caterpillar mining excavators was the 5130 Front Shovel (FS). Originally conceived at Caterpillar's MVC in Decatur, Illinois, along with the 793, 994, and 24H in the late 1980s, the 5130 was a totally new design. Instead of building an entire range of 5000-series models all at once, Caterpillar management and engineers decided to start with the market segment that could produce the largest sales potential, the 100-ton-capacity truck class. Since there were literally thousands of these trucks in service around the world at any given time, the 5130 would have an instant market. In this respect, the 5130 was designed from day one to perfectly match up to the 777C (95-ton capacity), and its eventual replacement, the 777D (100-ton capacity) with five-pass loading performance.

The 5130 Front Shovel design program and prototype build-up proceeded from 1989 to its eventual world unveiling in September at the 1992 MINExpo, held in Las Vegas, Nevada. The 5130 was more than two-and-a-half times larger than a 245B Series II excavator. The original design of the 5130 was equipped with an 11 cubic yard shovel bucket and was powered by a single Cat 3508 EUI, eight-cylinder, turbocharged and aftercooled diesel engine, rated at 700 flywheel-horsepower. This engine type could also be found in the 777C hauler and D11N dozer, which helped customers greatly when it came to stocking repair parts. Weight of the prototype unit was approximately 320,000 pounds. But after months of rigorous field testing of the early field trial units, changes were made to the excavator in early 1994 that greatly increased its performance and overall productivity. The 3508 Diesel Engine had its power increased to 755 flywheel-horsepower. Capacity of the front shovel bucket went up to 13¾ cubic yards, and castings and high-stress areas were beefed up. By the end of 1994, the 5130 now weighed in at 385,000 pounds for the front shovel, or almost 193 tons.

It would not be until late 1993 that a 5130 Mass Excavator (ME) configuration would be introduced into service. Equipped with either a 10.2 cubic yard dirt bucket, or a 17.8 cubic yard coal loading bucket, the 5130 ME proved to be a very productive and well-liked machine in the field. So much so that sales of the ME version soon eclipsed those of the FS model. The weight of the mass excavator was a bit more than the front shovel, with a fully operational unit coming in at 390,000 pounds.

This truck driver seems happy to be working with a big 992C, with its 12½ cubic yard bucket and Z Bar Linkage. Introduced in 1977, the 992C was equipped with a 690 flywheel-horsepower 3412 PCT engine. Caterpillar's 992 series of wheel loaders has endured for 35 years, since its inception in 1968, due to its outstanding performance and reliability.
Author's Collection

Above: A solid performer in the 195-ton class of mining trucks, this 789B Mining Truck was released in 1992 as an upgrade to the 789. It gets 1,705 flywheel-horsepower from its Cat 3516 EUI Diesel Engine, transferred to the wheels in a mechanical drivetrain. With nothing in the bed, the truck weighs just over 268,000 pounds. *Urs Peyer*

Right: A 773 Off-Highway Truck with bed at highest elevation is shown here in February 1972. Note the powerful hydraulic cylinders and the design fulcrum of the load. Released in 1970, the 773 was a 50-ton hauler with a 600-flywheel-horsepower engine. It was replaced in 1978 by the 773B, which added 10-tons to its load rating and another 50 horsepower in engine power. *Courtesy of Caterpillar Inc. Corporate Archives*

In 1997, a new 5130B variation was released with a host of improvements, including a boost in power, now up to 800 flywheel horsepower. Capacity was increased 14.5 cubic yards for the front shovel, bringing its weight up to 399,000 pounds. The 5130B ME version now weighed in at 401,000 pounds.

Not long after the 5130 started to find its way in the marketplace, Caterpillar introduced its second 5000-series excavator, the 5080. Much smaller than the 5130, the 5080 was in fact the front shovel version of the 375 Hydraulic Excavator. The 5080 made use of the 375's hydraulic systems, as well as its powerplant, the Cat 3406C ATAAC (Air-to-Air Aftercooled) turbocharged diesel engine, rated at 428 flywheel-horsepower. Though the main car body and undercarriage resembled those employed on the 375, they were suitably reinforced to withstand life as a front shovel in the 5080. Also of note, the operator's cab was raised substantially higher than that of the 375 to give the operator a more unobstructed view during the loading cycle. With a weight that ranges from 183,000 to 186,320 pounds and equipped with a 6.8 cubic yard bucket, the 5080 was perfectly matched to haul trucks in the 50-ton-capacity range. Because of its size, the 5080 was sized for aggregate work in the European marketplace. In 2002, the 5080 was replaced by the new 5090B front shovel, which was based heavily on the newly designed 385B excavator.

NEW GENERATION 307

With its large-capacity bowl and dual power, 550- to 605–flywheel-horsepower tractor engine, this tandem-engine Caterpillar 657E Wheel Tractor-Scraper is built for big jobs. Its scraper is harnessed to a 400- to 440-flywheel-horsepower engine and can be equipped with an auger for self-loading.
Caterpillar Inc.

NEW GENERATION

The Cat 990 Series II Wheel Loader with a standard lift arrangement is sized to load 50- to 70-ton trucks. With a high lift arrangement, this loader can also handle 100-ton trucks. Driven by a 625-flywheel-horsepower Cat 3412E Diesel Engine, the 990 offers bucket capacities from 11 to 12 cubic yards and a rated payload of 16½ tons. A high-pressure hydraulic system also allows rapid cycle times—9.2 seconds to raise, 2.9 seconds to dump, and 3.8 seconds to lower. *Nick Cedar*

In 2000, Caterpillar officially launched its 5110B Mass Excavator into the marketplace. The 5110B was sized between the 5080 and the 5130B. Powered by a Cat 3412E HEUI Diesel Engine, rated at 696 flywheel horsepower, and carrying a standard 9.9-cubic yard bucket, the 5110B was perfectly suited for loading trucks in the 50- to 60-ton capacity ranges, such as the Cat 773E and 775E. Weight of the 5110B in full operating trim is listed at 275,000 pounds.

Largest of all Caterpillar's mining excavators is the 5230 series. Originally introduced in 1994, the 5230 was designed to load haul trucks in the 150- to 240-ton range. The 5230 was almost twice the size of the 5130 at the time, and was capable of handling a 22.2-cubic yard bucket in front shovel form. The 5230 was equipped with a Cat 3516 EUI Diesel

Engine, rated at 1,470 flywheel-horsepower. In 1995, the 5230 ME (Mass Excavator) was released equipped with a standard bucket capacity of 20.3 cubic yards. In late 2001, an upgraded 5230B model was unveiled. Looking much like its predecessor, the new "B" variation was equipped with an improved, clean-burning Cat 3516B EUI Diesel Engine, now available with 1,550 flywheel-horsepower. Weight of the 5230B FS is listed at 721,000 pounds, with the ME version coming in at 723,400 pounds.

During the mid-1990s, a new design class of haulers began to appear in the marketplace, often referred to as ultrahaulers. Based on just a two-axle design, these trucks were typically capable of carrying 300-plus tons of material. Caterpillar had decided that they needed to be in the thick of things at the beginning of this new market push. Work began in earnest in early 1997 on the 797 project at Caterpillar's Mining and Construction Equipment Division in Decatur, Illinois. The entire truck was designed with 3D computer

A six-cylinder, direct injection, turbocharged and aftercooled diesel engine with four valves per cylinder produces 246 flywheel-horsepower to propel the 50,400-pound Cat 966G Wheel Loader. These loaders can be equipped with either a conventional steering wheel or Command Control Steering. The latter uses a pilot-operated, load-sensing system that controls the speed at which the machine turns in proportion to its steering wheel position. This offers precise control and quick response.

Nick Cedar

The largest wheel loader in the Caterpillar line, this 994 employs a 1,250-horsepower, 16-cylinder Caterpillar 3516 Diesel Engine. It left the factory weighing 390,300 pounds with a standard 23 cubic yard bucket rated for 35 tons, but the 994 had an optional 45 cubic yard bucket for loading coal. Its chassis could clear 2-foot boulders and dump a load from 20 feet, 4 inches high.
Caterpillar Inc.

technology, utilizing advanced finite element and solid entire component and structure designs that could be tested for fit and compatibility before any iron was machined.

One of the first issues that needed to be addressed was the engine type that would power the mammoth hauler. In the past, the company had a variety of diesel engines that could fit the needs of its equipment designs ready to go. But this situation was different. The 797 was going to require a powerplant that could produce well over 3,000 horsepower. In order to reach that power level, Caterpillar engineers combined two 3512B Diesel Engines, which were connected together by an innovative flexible coupling system that shared a common crankshaft. In this fashion, the engines would no longer function as two separate units but as one. The new diesel, to be known as the 3524B, was aftercooled with four single-stage turbochargers. Power ratings for this beast were a whopping 3,211 flywheel-horsepower.

On September 28, 1996, Caterpillar unveiled a truly astounding piece of engineering work—the massive 797 and its new engine. The 797 was not just big; it was truly huge. The 797 represented Cat engineering and manufacturing muscle at its finest. The truck alone used eight onboard computers to control and monitor all of its vital functions, and it could carry a payload of 360-plus tons of material. In all, the giant truck is 50 percent heavier than a fully loaded 747 jet airliner.

The load-bearing frame design of the 797 differs from that of the 793C hauler in that it is made up entirely of mild steel castings. Nine major castings are machined for a precise fit before being joined by robotic welders. The 793C uses a mixture of box-section steel structures, with steel castings in critical areas. The 797 frame design uses far fewer welds and creates a structure that is incredibly strong and suitable for supporting the kinds of loads the truck will face on a daily basis.

Another key factor in the design of the 797 is its use of 63-inch rims, one of the first in the industry. Previously, the largest rims available were 57 inches, the industry standard for haulers with more than 200-ton capacity. Caterpillar worked closely with Michelin on the development of the tires that would support the massive truck. The tires, new 55/80R63 radials, were simply the state of the art for haul trucks at the time of their development.

Weighing in at 76,700 pounds, the 330C L Hydraulic Excavator is powered by the Caterpillar C9 Diesel Engine, which is new to the excavator line. This six-cylinder, turbocharged diesel engine displaces 537 cubic inches and produces 247 net horsepower. This is approximately 11 percent more horsepower than the previous model, the 330B. The increased engine power also translates to an increased hydraulic flow of 17 percent compared to the previous model. Operation was simplified by eliminating work mode and power mode switches in the cab. Instead, the excavator chooses the best mode based on joystick movement.

Nick Cedar

A Caterpillar 785C waits to be filled under a Caterpillar 5230 Mass Excavator. The Caterpillar 785C payload is rated up to 150 tons, which it can carry at 34 miles per hour, driven by its 1,348-horsepower Cat 3512B diesel. The Cat 3512B EUI twin turbocharged and aftercooled Diesel Engine is a 12-cylinder, four-stroke design with a 23 percent torque rise for lugging up steep mining roads.
Caterpillar Inc.

The production development phase of the 797 program would start with approximately 20 units being built and put into service in various large mining operations, first in North America and then in South America.

In operation, the 797 rides and handles much like the company's other large mechanical-drive off-highway trucks. A loaded 797 has no problem pulling away from its loading area, even in less-than-ideal conditions. The engine's 3,211 flywheel-horsepower moves the truck out smartly and gets it up to speed quickly. The ride is exceptionally smooth, assisted in part by the operator's air-ride seat. The operator's ROPS cab has all the comforts of home, such as power windows, tilt-and-telescoping steering column, air conditioning, stereo, and

even a cup holder. On the dashboard is Caterpillar's vital information management system (VIMS) display and keypad, which provides precise machine status information to the operator during operation.

The cab is resiliently mounted to dampen noise and vibration. The cab also offers good lines of sight for the operator, and the clean design of the upper deck gives a clear view to the right of the truck. This is important, since the right-side rear-view mirror is almost 30 feet away from where the operator is sitting. An optional camera system is also available to allow the operator to see directly in front of and to the rear of the hauler.

Out in the field, the 797 has performed as expected. Improvements over time have included a reinforced frame, larger rear differential coolers, and new engine module frame design, and all of these improvements have added to the 797's overall operating weight of 1,345,000 pounds.

Introduced in 1992 to help meet the growing demand for versatile backhoe loaders, this multipurpose 436B can dig a hole over 16 feet deep and scoop up over a cubic yard of dirt. It has an 84-horsepower Cat diesel engine and an operating weight of 15,086 pounds. *Caterpillar Inc.*

One area of confusion about the 797 is its rated payload capacity. The hauler is rated at a nominal, or normal, capacity of 360-plus tons. But that "plus" is the real culprit here. A host of mine-specific conditions dictate how a 797 is set up. Haul road distance, grades out of the pit, weight of the material and geographic and weather conditions all play a part in determining the truck's ultimate working payload. Another factor that limits the hauler's tonnage capacity is its tires. Overloading of the 797 by over-enthusiastic mining operations has led to some premature tire wear. Heat buildup, caused by excessive loading, high travel speeds, and load haul distances, can shorten a tires life measurably. The heat buildup eventually leads to the breakdown of the sidewalls and carcass of the tire.

To help cope with extremes loads, Caterpillar offers the 797 with a standard flat-floor dump body, or special mine-specific-design (MSD) bodies. These dump bodies can be fabricated to meet a host of material hauling needs. Lighter-weight bodies can be specified for less abrasive material. In doing this, weight subtracted from the dump bodies' design adds directly to the payload capacity of the truck. Other designs have different floor configurations. In Wyoming, 797 haulers, equipped with specially designed coal bodies fabricated by WOTCO of Casper, Wyoming, regularly average 380 to 386 tons per trip. Designed for hauling coal, their voluminous 588 cubic yard bodies are simply huge, especially when compared to the standard 290 cubic yard box. This capacity is possible since coal is a lighter-weight material, so it takes more of it to reach the trucks' rated payload capacity.

In the spring of 2002, Caterpillar announced the release of the 797B. The 797B hauler had its load capacity increased to a nominal 380 tons. To cope with the extra payload capacity, power output was increased to 3,370 flywheel-horsepower. Another big improvement to the haulers all around productivity are its new Michelin advanced low-profile 59/80R63 radial tires, which are the largest truck tires currently available in the world. With all of these improvements, the 797B now tips the scales fully loaded at 1,375,000 pounds. The first 797B haulers were officially dedicated into service in October 2002 at an oil sands mining operation located in Northern Alberta.

In 1996, Caterpillar officially introduced the D11N Tractor's replacement, the D11R. The D11R (8ZR) featured a host of evolutionary improvements that would continue with the sales success story of the D11N, which claimed approximately 70 percent of the world's large dozer sales in its size class. Though the D11R looked like the former D11N model (except for its new black operator's cab), a host of new features improved reliability and increased operator comfort and productivity. These improvements included hallmarks that made Caterpillar the number one producer of heavy equipment worldwide. Some of the key improvements included thicker brake plates and increased oil flow; an electronic clutch brake (ECB) steering system with fingertip control (FTC); an improved multiple row module (IMRM) radiator; and a Caterpillar monitoring system (CMS) with track odometer.

Of all these improvements, the electronic clutch brake (ECB) steering system with low effort fingertip control (FTC) was the biggest change. This system combined steering,

A 350 L Hydraulic Excavator with a demolition attachment picks up scrap metal after a take-down. Cat produces a line of optional demolition and sorting attachments such as the grapple shown in this photo. Introduced in 1993, the 350 L has a 286 flywheel-horsepower Cat diesel engine and can lift just over 20 tons.
Urs Peyer

Caterpillar designed the 793C Mining Truck to achieve the lowest cost-per-ton hauling in mining applications with the ability to carry a 502,000-pound target payload. Unlike many competitors, Caterpillar uses a mechanical powertrain. This allows an efficient use of power, and an overall efficiency of between 82 and 85 percent is maintained up to 15 percent effective grade. The 2,166 flywheel-horsepower, 16-cylinder engine, six-speed power-shift transmission, and brake system share information over the CAT Data Link. This allows the components to work together as a system.
Nick Cedar

machine direction, and gear selection into a control system clustered to the operator's left. The system could be operated with one hand and with minimal effort, allowing for superior operator comfort and increased productivity. Blade and ripper controls were mounted to the right of the operator's seat.

The engine and power output ratings of the D11R were the same as the D11N. Bulldozing blades and capacities were also unchanged from the previous model. Weight was up a bit, reaching 216,963 pounds when equipped with the full U-blade and single shank ripper. The heaviest combination was the 11U abrasion blade package with multi-shank ripper, which tipped the scales at 225,903 pounds.

The early D11R might have disappointed a few because it maintained the old D11N's power output and blade capacities. But this was merely the first installment of what Caterpillar had up its sleeve concerning its top-of-the-line dozer. In September 1996, at the MINExpo '96 mining show held in Las Vegas, Nevada, the company unveiled a second model of its famous track-type tractor—the D11R Carrydozer.

The D11R Carrydozer (CD) was not a replacement or upgrade of the standard D11R. It was a second model type with a completely new blade design. The D11R CD (9XR) was primarily designed for large-volume production dozing in prime mine stripping and land reclamation projects. The new dozer's blade carried material inside the blade curvature for increased productivity. Material carried in the blade also allowed operation of the D11R CD on steeper slopes. Blade capacity of the Carrydozer was 57 cubic yards, 12 more than the standard D11R. The blade of the Carrydozer measured 22 feet in width, and 10 feet, 8 inches in height to the top of the rock guard.

Engineers also saw fit to install an improved Cat 3508B EUI Diesel Engine under the hood. The B-model of this engine meets tougher government standards concerning lower noise and emission levels. The new D11R CD now boasted a power output of 850 flywheel-horsepower. In operation, the D11R will run out of traction long before it ever runs out of

Electronically controlled Caterpillar engines allow the 140H and 160H Motor Graders to operate more cleanly and quietly than previous models. The motor graders generate exterior sound levels of less than 109 decibels when equipped with a sound suppression package. The sound level in the cabs is 75 decibels. Both models can be equipped with VHP or VHP Plus, which restricts power when traction is limited and increases power in higher gears when more power is needed. The 140H pictured offers a power range from 165 to 185 horsepower.
Nick Cedar

A monument to Caterpillar engineering, the 797 Off-Highway Truck was one of the first major pieces of equipment designed using Caterpillar's virtual design center. Before the first part was cast, it was thoroughly tested in computer-generated quarries in a sophisticated virtual-reality theater. The 797 is powered by a Cat 3524B EUI producing 3,400 horsepower, using 65 gallons of fuel per hour and averaging 0.3 miles per gallon. Due to these operating costs, the 797 usually runs 24 hours per day, 365 days per year, stopping only for regularly scheduled maintenance. There are no fewer than eight onboard computers to monitor oil pressure, transmission torque, engine performance, and tire temperature. Behind each wheel is a pack of 42-inch brake discs. Dissipating that energy is a computer controlled brake-cooling system that pumps oil through multiple coolers and then back through the discs.
Caterpillar Inc.

power. In fact, with an extremely full blade, the tracks will slip and crawl as they constantly bite into the ground, but the engine never misses a beat, never strains, and is never wanting for more power.

Other performance-enhancing improvements found on the D11R CD included a beefed up frame, extra-heavy-duty single-shank ripper carriage, and new low-effort electro-hydraulic dozer controls. The ripper and implement controls were now all electronic. Also, an optional computer-aided earthmoving system (CAES) was offered that guided the operator's dozing patterns with the aid of a global positioning system (GPS).

As one might expect, all of these new features and designs would add just a bit of weight to the tractor's mass. Weighing in at 239,550 pounds in full operating trim, it is even heavier than the old D11N equipped with the giant impact ripper. At the time of its introduction, the Carrydozer was only offered with a single-shank ripper. If the ripper is not required, then a 29,620 pound counterweight is installed to maintain the tractor's overall balance. The D11R CD had limited availability throughout 1997 as it went through its test phase. Full production would officially get under way by April 1998.

In August 1997, Caterpillar released an updated version of the standard D11R, which featured many of the improvements first seen on the new Carrydozer model a few months earlier. The standard D11R (9TR) now featured the 850-flywheel-horsepower engine, including the new cooling system, stronger mainframe, and improved undercarriage and dozer structures. Standard operating weight of the dozer with full U-blade and single-shank ripper was now listed at 222,133 pounds, with the 11U ABR blade and multishank model coming in at 228,598 pounds.

Entering the next century, the D11R and the D11R CD are the most powerful and productive track-type crawlers ever offered by Caterpillar. In late 1999, Caterpillar saw fit to add even more upgrades and features to the big dozers to make them even more productive. The D11R (7PZ) and D11R CD (AAF) now featured an optional environmental cab with a host of interior changes, including a new Comfort Series seat. The latest in controls, including the vital information display system (VIDS) and computer-aided earthmoving system (CAES) can also be found on the dozers. With CAES, the operator is given an in-cab, real-time work plan, which is continually updated to indicate where to cut and fill.

NEW GENERATION 323

Also, the Carrydozer could now be optioned with a multishank ripper. All of these changes added just a bit more weight to these high-end production dozers, with the standard D11R now coming in at 230,100 pounds, and the D11R CD at 248,600 pounds, the heaviest of any track-type tractor in Caterpillar's history. In addition to the other enhancements mentioned, the Carrydozer would also receive further improvements in October 2000 with the addition of a strengthened main frame and a new tag link design, which now attached the link to the blade instead of the push arms. This made sure that blade side loads were now applied directly to the main frame to ensure a long connector life.

In the late 1980s, as mining operations began to employ larger fleets of large-capacity off-highway haulers, their haul road infrastructures were becoming more and more of a concern. Good haul roads were of the most importance to mine operators. As haul trucks increased in capacity, their overall size and weight also increased exponentially. Though mining operations could make due with motor graders in the size class of a 16-series

This 240-ton-capacity Caterpillar 793C Mining Truck is designed to reduce a mining operation's cost-per-ton through high production. Its 2,166-horsepower, Caterpillar 3516B high-displacement diesel engine is run by computer, which continually analyzes sensor data for engine monitoring, control, and protection. Braking the truck's 830,000-pound working weight heading downhill is a feat of technology. Inside the 793C's four-wheel, forced-oil-cooled, multiple-disc brakes, an oil film prevents direct contact between the discs, absorbing braking forces and slowing the truck by shearing oil molecules. The heat generated is transferred to the oil and carried away to oil coolers, extending brake life. Integrated into the overall braking system, an engine retarder helps slow the 793C and reduce brake wear by running against compression on downhill hauls. *Caterpillar Inc.*

machine, they required the use of a small fleet of them, each requiring its own operator in multiple shifts. Caterpillar soon realized that what its mining customers needed was not more motor graders, but larger and more productive units that could take the place of multiple machines. After the concept was refined, Cat engineers started to work on what would eventually become the 24H.

Like its other mining equipment cousins, the 994 loader and the 793 hauler, the 24H started its life at Cat's Mining Vehicle Center. With haulers soon to be introduced to the mining industry in excess of 300 tons capacity, Caterpillar engineers calculated that a grader with blade dimensions of 24 feet would soon be needed. By 1994, the overall design of the 24H was locked in stone and construction began on the first prototype.

Introduced in 1994, the 5230 Front Shovel is powered by a sixteen-cylinder Cat 3516 EUI quad-turbocharged and aftercooled diesel engine, with an output of 1,470 flywheel-horsepower and 1,575 gross horsepower. This machine weighs 692,320 pounds and with its 20.3 cubic yard bucket, it should be able to fill that 789C in five passes.
Eric C. Orlemann

At its introduction at the MINExpo mega-show in 1996, the 992G caused a sensation with its dramatic one-piece, cast-steel, box-section lift boom, a bold departure from the twin-steel-plate designs of past wheel loaders. Innovative in nearly all areas of design, from its hydraulics to its cooling system, the 992G is a truly impressive machine.

Urs Peyer

The 24H was designed for mining operations that utilize 150-ton capacity and larger haul trucks. Its principle task was to build and maintain haul roads. Unlike the 16H grader, which was designed to do a broad range of grading and ditching applications, the 24H was built as the ultimate management tool for the mining industry, where larger haul roads were of a concern. The 24H can do the work of two 16H graders. Even though the 24H cost considerably more than the 16H, its lower cost per haul and low maintenance made it cost-effective.

The 24H achieved this impressive production output with power, weight, and one mighty big blade. The 24H is powered by a rear mounted 12-cylinder Cat 3412E HEUI, turbocharged diesel engine, rated at 500 flywheel-horsepower. Though some Caterpillar grader models offer six-wheel drive capabilities, only the rear tandems are driven on the 24H. The frame of the grader is articulated just behind the cab, giving the unit enhanced maneuverability in tight working situations. An optional rear-mounted ripper with up to seven ripping shanks is also available. Overall working weight is listed at 136,611 pounds, more than twice that of the 16H. With this type of power and weight, the 24H can apply greater cutting forces to its blade, enabling it to take on the most difficult road surfaces.

The business end of the 24H is its standard 24-foot long moldboard. This blade, which measures 42 inches in height, has the ability to move almost 2½ times the material the 16H can. In fact, the 24H produces 40 percent greater down pressure on the blade than the 16H. And with the 24H's wider blade, the grader makes fewer passes to do the same job a 16H would do with its 16-foot blade. A blade the size of the 24H is essential for the economical road building duties within mine sites. As a rule of thumb, two-way haul roads need to be three to four times the width of the trucks being used. And with mining haulers such as the 797 measuring 30 feet across, the roadways that need to be built to service trucks like these are huge.

Caterpillar delivered its first preproduction 24H in late 1995. Other units were placed throughout North America for field follow-through testing. The 24H was officially released for worldwide availability around May 1996. This was done so its production and marketing could be integrated with the other large mining equipment product lines also being built at the plant.

Designed from the ground up as the replacement for the 992D Wheel Loader, the 992G broke new technological design ground for the company in 1996. What made the 992G loader unique was its utilization of a one-piece, cast-steel, box-section front lift arm design, instead of the former twin-boom configuration. This new front-end had three times the strength of the previous model. Stresses were spread over the entire boom into the frame and not through weld joints. Though the idea of a mono-boom concept was not necessarily new to the industry, it had previously been utilized only on smaller machines, never on one the size of the 992G.

Along with the newly designed front end of the 992G, a host of other features also stand out. The structures on the loader were more than 90 percent robotically welded, for highly consistent welds with deep plate penetration and fusion, resulting in increased strength. The new box-section frame of the 992G is extended further forward, improving rail-to-hitch strength and giving the working platform more stability and balance. Mounted in the rear of the loader is a more powerful and cleaner burning eight-cylinder Cat 3508B EUI, twin-turbocharged and aftercooled diesel engine, which is rated at 800 flywheel-horsepower.

With all of these changes and extra power on hand, the loader's capacity also increased. The 992G's bucket capacity ranged from 15 to 16 cubic yards, depending on the specific application of the unit. Equipped with the 16 cubic yard large standard spade edge bucket, it was a perfectly sized machine for the loading of 100-ton-capacity haulers. In fact it could load the Caterpillar 777D in four quick passes. Equipped with the 16 cubic yard bucket, the 992G weighed 202,499 pounds in full operating trim, with the high-lift version coming in at 209,373 pounds. Caterpillar officially released the new loader for sale to the world earthmoving marketplace in March 1997.

A close cousin to the 992G Wheel Loader in Caterpillar's vast product lines is the 854G Wheel Dozer. The 854G can track its beginnings with a prototype wheel dozer that was first displayed at the 1996 MINExpo called the Tiger 790G. An Australian firm, Tiger Engineering Pty, Ltd., with the assistance of Caterpillar Industrial Products, had been involved with the production of large rubber-tired wheel dozers based on Caterpillar drive-trains and various other components, especially from the Cat 992C Wheel Loader, since 1980. Tiger delivered its first wheel dozer, the 690A in 1982. In 1985, they introduced their 690B, which utilized the torque converter from the Cat 773B Off-Highway Truck. 1n 1993, Tiger introduced the 690D not long after Caterpillars release of the 992D Wheel Loader. The Tiger dozers were sold and serviced by Caterpillar's worldwide dealer network, which made the decision in 1997 by Caterpillar to buy the design and manufacturing rights to the 790G, as well as the smaller Tiger dozers, all the more easier. In March 1998, the new wheel dozers were officially released for sale as Caterpillar products bearing the new nomenclature of 854G, which was based on the 992G, and the 844, which was based on the 990 Series II Wheel Loader.

The 854G is one of the largest full production wheel dozers manufactured today. Power for such a large dozer is supplied by a Cat 3508B EUI Diesel Engine, rated at 800 flywheel-horsepower. The business end of the 854G is its massive dozing blade. Three types are available: a semi-U-blade, and a heavy-duty semi-U-blade, both rated at 33.1 cubic yards; and a coal stockpiling blade rated at 58.2 cubic yards. Working weight of the 854G equipped with the heavy-duty blade is 220,424 pounds. With this kind of power and weight, the 854G has become a common sight in large open pit mining operations around the world, where its versatility and speed are unmatched by anything else in its class today.

Here, a fighting D8N is loaded onto a Lockheed C-5A Galaxy in 1991, headed for Kuwait and the First Gulf War. The tractor's 82,590-pound weight is no problem. The C-5A can handle up to three of them.
Caterpillar Inc.

This 631G Wheel Tractor–Scraper's Cat 3408E Diesel Engine is dual powered, providing an extra 40 horsepower in higher gear for faster road speed (up to 33 miles per hour). It also comes equipped with a power-shift transmission with eight gears forward and one in reverse. The scraper was designed to lower cost per cubic yard in medium to large projects with its 31 cubic yard (heaped) open-bowl scraper blade.
Caterpillar Inc.

This Caterpillar 135H Motor Grader has a 12-by-2-foot blade and a turning radius of just 23.8 feet. Its six-cylinder powerplant is a Cat 3126B DITA ATAAC VHP, displacing 439 cubic inches with 169 gross horsepower and a maximum torque of 625 ft-lb.

Fully loaded, the 135H weighs 40,263 pounds and can reach a top speed of 26.1 miles per hour, 20.6 miles per hour in reverse.
Caterpillar Inc.

With an operating weight of 83,500 pounds, the D8R draws power from a Caterpillar 3406E Diesel Engine that pumps out 310 net horsepower. This engine is mated to a power-shift transmission and a torque divider that offers the benefits of a direct-drive powertrain while maintaining the benefits of a converter drive. The electronic engine and transmission controls communicate to allow the powertrain to operate more efficiently.

Nick Cedar

Above: Push loading scrapers is often an efficient method to move large volumes of earth. Here a 310 net horsepower D8R Series II Tractor is used to help push load a 621G Wheel Tractor-Scraper with a Cat 3406E Diesel Engine that produces variable 330/365 flywheel-horsepower. The 621G cuts a path 9 feet, 11 inches wide and up to 13.1 inches deep. The scraper is capable of moving a 20 cubic yard heaped capacity in a single pass.
Nick Cedar

Right: The Caterpillar 797B Off-Highway Truck is the largest mining truck in the world, with an operating weight of 1,375,000 pounds and a payload capacity of 380 tons.
Gary Middlebrook

The D11R Track-Type Tractor has a more powerful engine than its predecessor, with a 25 percent net torque rise for better lugging performance.
Eric C. Orlemann

Workers perform final paint detail on the mammoth D11R Track-Type Tractor at Caterpillar's plant in East Peoria, Illinois. *Eric C. Orlemann*

This 994D is a recent (1998) update to Caterpillar's largest line of wheel loaders, the 994 series. Its four-plate loader arms can hoist a 38-ton payload, designed for efficient loading with a 785C or a 789C. It has a 1,250-horsepower, 16-cylinder Cat 3516B EUI Diesel Engine displacing 4,221 cubic inches (nearly 2½ cubic feet).
Caterpillar Inc.

NEW GENERATION

While not as big as the mammoth 24H, this 16H Motor Grader is still considered a large, high-production machine. It has a six-cylinder, 275 flywheel-horsepower Cat 3406 TA Diesel Engine, a power-shift transmission and load-sensing hydraulics that are well integrated into one machine. Its 16-foot moldboard can reach a top speed of nearly 28 miles per hour.
Eric C. Orlemann

At its introduction in 1996, the 24H Motor Grader was the largest motor grader offered for sale in the world, designed to build and maintain mining roads. It has a twelve-cylinder, 500-flywheel-horsepower Cat 3412E Diesel Engine, which can move the motor grader's 136,610 pounds at 23.4 miles per hour. The 24H is equipped with a 24-foot moldboard with several optional cutting edges.

Eric C. Orlemann

A 119 maximum flywheel-horsepower Cat 3126B HEUI Diesel Engine powers the D5N. An elevated sprocket undercarriage is designed for optimal balance and performance in fine grading to heavy dozing applications. Finger Tip Control (FTC) combines steering, machine direction, and gear selection into a single, one-hand operated system. A cab, air conditioning, and a suspension seat are all standard equipment.

Nick Cedar

Wheel dozers combine the production capabilities of tracked dozers with the versatility and mobility of wheel loaders. The 844 pictured weighs 155,120 pounds and produces 620 flywheel-horsepower. It is engineered for large dozing applications. Mated to a 17-foot, 4-inch semi-U blade, the dozer has a 21.1 cubic yard capacity. Articulated frame steering makes possible a 7-foot, 4-inch turning circle with the blade. With three forward and three reverse speeds, the 844 has a 13-mile-per-hour top speed.

Nick Cedar

The D7R Series II performs a wide range of functions, from finish grading to production dozing. Three different undercarriages allow the D7R Series II to be tailored to a given application. The D7R Series II has an operating weight of 54,582 pounds when equipped with the standard undercarriage and produces 240 net horsepower. Bulldozer blades range in capacity from 5.08 cubic yards to 10.91 cubic yards. An adjustable multishank ripper or a hydraulically powered winch add to the versatility.
Nick Cedar

The Caterpillar 314C LCR Hydraulic Excavator has a compact radius design, which makes this the ideal machine for operators who work in space-restricted areas. The tail swing radius is 4 feet, 10 inches. This allows the machine to swing in tight spaces. Depending on how it is equipped, the 314C LCR can weigh up to 32,650 pounds. A Caterpillar 3064T Diesel Engine produces 90 net horsepower. When equipped with the long stick, it has a 19 foot, 6 inch maximum digging depth.
Nick Cedar

At 105,080 pounds, with a package height, length and width of 12'1"x38'6"x9'10", this 345BL is an excellent medium-size excavator. With its 290 flywheel-horsepower Cat diesel engine driving its hydraulic pump at full throttle, it can lift over 23 tons. Released in 1998, the 345BL had a three-year production life before it was replaced by the Series II model.

Urs Peyer

The Cat 163H Motor Grader's all-wheel drive improves tractive effort in poor underfoot conditions. The grader, which uses a 14-foot-wide blade, features a Caterpillar 3176C Diesel Engine with variable horsepower (VHP). It produces up to 180 net horsepower in gears 1 to 3 and up to 200 net horsepower in gears 4 to 8. This engine works with the eight-speed forward/six-speed reverse power-shift transmission and load-sensing hydraulics to deliver maximum productivity.

Nick Cedar

The Cat CS-563E Compactor weighs 24,520 pounds with a 12,877-pound weight at the drum and compacts an 84-inch width. Its 60-inch-diameter drum transmits a maximum 60,000-pound centrifugal force. Direct hydrostatic drive propels Cat compactors and provides maximum gradeability.
Nick Cedar

The Cat CS-583E Compactor is powered by a 143-flywheel-horsepower Cat 3056E Diesel Engine and weighs 33,296 pounds with a weight at the drum of 21,741 pounds. Its 60-inch-diameter drum compacts an 80-inch width and produces a maximum centrifugal force of 74,600 pounds.

Nick Cedar

The Caterpillar 777D is a versatile workhorse serving heavy construction, industrial, mining, and quarry/aggregate applications. It is equipped with a Mega 20,000 water truck body to keep dust under control on mining sites. This reliable production truck uses a high-torque-rise Caterpillar 3508B Diesel Engine that produces 938 flywheel-horsepower to propel the target 100-ton payload up to 37.5 miles per hour. An optional traction control system monitors wheel slip and automatically applies the oil-cooled wet disc brakes to slow a spinning wheel if slip exceeds the set limit.
Nick Cedar

With a payload rated up to 720,000 pounds, the Caterpillar 797 Off-Highway Truck reigned as the world's largest at its introduction in the year 1999. It sits on 13-foot-tall 55/80R63 Michelin radial tires, specially designed for the 797 and costing approximately $30,000 each, mounted on 63-inch rims. These support a working mass, fully loaded, of 1.23 million pounds and roll along at speeds up to 40 miles per hour. A new 797 arrives from Caterpillar in pieces on 12 semitrailers, including its 850-gallon (or optional 1,800-gallon) fuel tank.

Caterpillar Inc.

The D11R Track-Type Tractor was introduced in March 1996, powered by a Cat 3508B Diesel Engine rated at 850 flywheel-horsepower. The V-8, four-stroke, turbocharged and aftercooled Cat 3508B displaces over 2,100 cubic inches, with a bore and stroke of 6.7x7.5 inches. It uses 28 gallons of oil.
Caterpillar Inc.

A Caterpillar D11R pulls a scraper to its next job. This tractor operates at a weight of 230,100 pounds and can be configured with a counterweight. Its vital information display system (VIDS) continuously monitors the D11R's systems and alerts the operator to abnormal conditions.
Caterpillar Inc.

The tandem-engine 657E Wheel Tractor-Scraper, Caterpillar's largest, has a bowl capacity of 32 cubic yards struck, 44 cubic yards heaped, and can reach speeds of 31.1 miles per hour at a total operating weight of 159,226 pounds. It can carry 415 gallons of fuel to feed its total of 20 engine-block cylinders, 12 in the tractor's Cat 3412E, and 8 in the scraper's Cat 3408.
Caterpillar Inc.

This D11R Carrydozer, named for its uniquely shaped blade capable of moving a vast 57 cubic yards of material, is a high-production machine for mining operations. Its Cat 3508B Diesel Engine is fed by a 425-gallon fuel tank and lubricated with 28 gallons of oil. At an operating weight of 248,600 pounds, the 850 horsepower D11R Carrydozer has a six-gear transmission (three forward and three reverse) that can reach an overall top speed of 8.7 miles per hour.

Caterpillar Inc.

The Cat 330B Log Loader is a purpose-built machine with 247 flywheel-horsepower, designed to meet the rigors of forestry work. In the log load under configuration, this 97,973-pound machine is capable of reaching out 43 feet.
Nick Cedar

Designed for just the sort of trenching and pipe-laying job shown in this photo, this 385BL Hydraulic Excavator's advanced hydraulics sustain a productive pace. Its 258 gallon/minute, main hydraulic circuit utilizes Cat's load-sensing, Proportional Priority Pressure Compensated (PPPC) system to make the 385BL bucket controls responsive to the operator, not the load. The 385BL weighs 183,940 pounds and is powered by a turbocharged and aftercooled Cat 3456 ATAAC Diesel Engine, capable of delivering 513 flywheel horsepower.

Urs Peyer

NEW GENERATION

With the momentum from the very successful launch of the 5130 Front Shovel in 1992, Caterpillar followed up with the 5130B Front Shovel in July 1997 (5130B ME—Mass Excavator—version shown in this photo). More capacity and power were built into the new package, with a bucket capacity of 13.7 cubic yards and an eight-cylinder, 800-flywheel-horsepower Cat 3508B, with a displacement of 2,105 cubic inches.

The hydraulic system uses 476 gallons of fluid, with a maximum flow of 99 gallons/minute up to a pressure of 4500 psi.
Urs Peyer

This high-production 5090B Front Shovel has no time to take in the view. A solid performer in Caterpillar's current product line, the 5090B is rated at 513 flywheel-horsepower. Maximum bucket capacity is 7.4 cubic yards. Overall working weight is 192,900 pounds.

Urs Peyer

With short to moderate haul distances, wheel tractor-scrapers such as the 20 cubic yard heaped capacity Caterpillar 627G are often the most cost-efficient way to move large quantities of earth. This production machine cuts a 9-foot, 11-inch swath at a maximum cut depth of 13.1 feet. Two Caterpillar engines, a 330/365-horsepower 3406E on the tractor and a 225-horsepower 3306 on the scraper, provide the necessary force to load the bowl and then transport its payload at speeds up to 32 miles per hour.
Nick Cedar

CHAPTER 10
THE NEXT CENTURY

As the new century unfolds, Caterpillar finds itself with one of the largest and most varied product line offerings ever in its history. Some of these categories include the well established blood lines of the company, such as track-type tractors, track loaders, wheel loaders, wheel dozers, landfill and soil compactors, hydraulic excavators, wheel-tractor scrapers, motor graders, articulated and off-highway trucks. Newer offerings include skid steer, multi terrain, and backhoe loaders, telehandlers, demolition and wheel excavators, track and wheel material handlers, log loaders, track feller bunchers, wheel and track skidders, vibratory soil, pneumatic, and asphalt compactors, cold planers, road reclaimers, asphalt paving equipment, and underground mining equipment. As for engines, Caterpillar is a world leader in the design and production of heavy-duty diesel engines of all size types and power outputs that power today's trucks, buses, ships, and locomotives. Caterpillar also offers one of the most complete lines of generator sets for every application thinkable. The list goes on and on.

As already mentioned, Caterpillar over the years has expanded its product offerings greatly through strategic manufacturing alliances with other companies, as well as through acquisitions of existing firms, such as Russell, Trackson, Mitsubishi, DJB, and Tiger Engineering. But these firms are only part of the story. Others have also played a part in making Caterpillar the undisputed global heavy-weight champ in industrial equipment design and manufacturing today.

Caterpillar Engine Division was greatly enhanced in 1981 with the purchase of Solar Turbines Industrial Division of International Harvester Company, which added a full range of massive and powerful gas turbine powerplants. In 1996, the German firm of MaK Motoren GmbH was added, bring with it a host of new diesel engine designs. In December 1997, Caterpillar agreed to the purchase of the British firm of Perkins, one of the world leaders in the production of smaller diesel engines, from Lucas Varity Plc. With these purchases, Caterpillar was now able to control the production of virtually all of the engines powering its equipment offerings today.

Paving equipment offerings first appeared in Caterpillar's product lines in 1984, when it entered a manufacturing and marketing agreement with the CMI Corporation of Oklahoma. Even though this association was discontinued in 1987, Caterpillar was able to purchase from CMI the technology to manufacture pavement profilers, asphalt pavers, soil stabilizers, and road reclaimers. They were also able to purchase CMI's wholly owned subsidiary, RayGo, Inc., of Minnesota, which added a broad range of soil and asphalt compactors. But the big news in these offerings was Caterpillar's purchase of Barber-Greene in April 1991, which would add a complete asphalt paving equipment line up. This would help round out Caterpillar's product offerings concerning paving products, making it one of the most complete in the world.

The R1700 Series II is one of a number of underground mining machines produced by Elphinstone, a wholly owned subsidiary of Caterpillar.
Caterpillar Inc.

Material can be spread and dumped on the go without raising the body of this Caterpillar 740 Ejector Articulated Truck. This addresses a stability concern on many construction sites with conventional articulated truck bodies that have more of a tendency to roll over when they are raised on uneven terrain. In addition, spreading material while the truck is moving cuts cycle times, and the ejector mechanism prevents materials from sticking to the inside of the truck body.
Nick Cedar

Caterpillar equipment can be found in surface mining operations all over the globe. Now it can be found underground as well. In 1995 Caterpillar entered into a joint venture company with Dale B. Elphinstone Pty. Ltd. of Tasmania, Australia. The new company, Caterpillar Elphinstone Pty. Ltd., produced underground mining equipment utilizing Caterpillar drivetrains and components. This included low-profile Load-Haul-Dump (LHD) loaders, and rigid frame and articulated haulers. In 2000, Caterpillar officially acquired the remaining 50 percent of the joint venture company, now making all "Elphies" produced, 100 percent Caterpillar designed and manufactured. Currently, Caterpillar Elphinstone offers six models of underground haul trucks, as well as six models of LHD loaders to choose from.

In 1998, Caterpillar announced the release of a new line of compact machines sized for the smaller contractor, as well as rental fleets. Designed and built by Caterpillar, the first offerings were mini hydraulic excavators and compact wheel loaders. In January 1999, skid steer loaders were officially introduced into the North American marketplace. Of all these new releases, the skid steer machines have caused the most excitement. These tough and versatile loader types have been in the marketplace for years, but this was the first time Caterpillar had offered one of its own. With their simple joystick controls, skid steering, and the ability to accept a wide range of work tools, such as augers, landscape tillers, trenchers, brooms, buckets, and forks, they are a contractors dream come true.

The Caterpillar 740 Articulated Truck can carry a rated 42-ton payload with its 30 cubic yard heaped (SAE 2:1) capacity body at speeds up to 34.2 miles per hour. A three-point front suspension oscillates plus or minus 6 degrees to allow the operator to travel faster over rough terrain while the rear uses a stable walking beam suspension. Oil-immersed, multiplate brakes provide stopping power and long life.
Nick Cedar

Two engines power this 637G up steep grades and enable all-wheel drive to handle soft, slippery conditions. Both are dual-power engines, the tractor engine providing an extra 35 horsepower in gears 3 through 8 for a total of 490 net horsepower. The new 637G features a redesigned bowl with a 10 percent increase in capacity over the 657F (31 cubic yards heaped, 21 cubic yards struck) and better load retention (82,260 pounds rated). The low-profile design of the bowl offers less resistance to incoming materials, while cellular construction adds strength and dent resistance to bowl sides and floor.

Caterpillar Inc.

Currently, there are ten models available, ranging from 48 to 74 flywheel-horsepower. If a model with a bit more traction is required, Caterpillar offers the multi terrain loaders. Based on its new skid steer machines, the multi terrain loaders are equipped with a special rubber tracked undercarriage developed by ASV Inc. of Grand Rapids, Minnesota. In late 2000, Caterpillar purchased a 15 percent share of the ASV Company. At the same time, both companies signed an alliance agreement in which they would jointly develop and manufacture a new line of rubber track skid steer loaders. Referred to as multi terrain loaders, the first units would enter the marketplace in 2001. Currently, five models are offered, ranging from 54 to 74 flywheel-horsepower. Key advantages of the suspended rubber-tracked Maximum Traction and Support System Undercarriage, (MTSS) is its superior traction in all types of conditions, low ground pressure to reduce soil compaction, and high flotation for working in soft underfoot conditions.

Caterpillar is constantly improving and diversifying all of its product lines to meet current and future customer expectations. But there are times when a product line no longer fits within the company's long term strategic plans. This was the case with the Challenger tractors. It was decided that the design and manufacture of agricultural equipment was not in the long-term best interests of the company. In December 2001, Caterpillar announced that it was going to sell its Challenger MT tractor line to AGCO Corporation of Duluth, Georgia. This included the design, assembly, and marketing of the MT-series ag tractors, with Caterpillar acting as a supplier of parts and provide technical support to AGCO. The deal was finalized in the first part of 2002. Then in December 2002, Caterpillar announced it was selling its rubber-belted track component business, including the plant located in Emporia, Kansas, to Camoplast of Sherbrooke, Quebec, Canada. Camoplast is a leading world supplier of rubber-belt drive technology for all types of applications, including agriculture machines and recreation snowmobiles. The Canadian company would now supply AGCO with undercarriages for the MT-series Challenger line.

With a flywheel horsepower of 365, a capacity of 14 cubic yards struck, 20 heaped, and a top speed, fully loaded, of 32 miles per hour, the Caterpillar 621G Wheel Tractor-Scraper is a worthy replacement for the 621F. Its electronically controlled Caterpillar diesel engine distributes torque through an improved powertrain. Optional on the 621G is a bowl auger system, which extends capability as well as capacity (to 21 cubic yards).
Caterpillar Inc.

The Caterpillar 623G self-loading, elevating scraper shown here has a capacity of 18 cubic yards struck, 23 heaped. It features 365 flywheel-horsepower and a top speed, fully loaded, of 32 miles per hour. *Caterpillar Inc.*

Throughout the 1980s and 1990s, Caterpillar added and refined its heavy equipment offerings. One of these new standout product lines developed during this time period was the backhoe loaders. Originally introduced in 1985, the backhoe loaders were a major effort by Caterpillar at the time to diversify its product offerings to smaller contractor sized businesses and rental fleets, and not just be seen as a builder of large, heavy-duty earthmoving machines. Designed and manufactured by Caterpillar, the first model introduced was the 62 flywheel-horsepower 416. This model would soon be joined by others, including four-wheel-drive, all-wheel-steering designed loaders. The most powerful backhoe loader offered by the company today is its 446B, rated at 102 flywheel-horsepower.

Another of the company's standout product lines is its articulated haulers. The worldwide articulated hauler marketplace is a very completive place to say the least. Because of the extreme conditions the articulated hauler works in, designs that are not up to it, quickly go the way of the dinosaur. Caterpillar's offerings in this group are ranked near the top as some of the finest and most productive articulated haulers built today. But to stay completive, updates and new model introductions are the order of things. Manufacturers that rest on their laurels in this marketplace soon find themselves at the back of the class. Starting in 2000, Caterpillar began introducing new articulated trucks bearing the new 700-series product line identification. The first two models released were the 25-ton capacity 725 and the 30-ton 730. These would be followed in 2001 by the 35-ton 735 and 40-ton 740. All models featured extra heavy-duty drivetrains with six-wheel drive, and

This Caterpillar 627G is a tandem-powered wheel tractor–scraper with extra power for rough going. It was designed to reduce construction costs on projects under a half-million cubic yards, and it can be configured with an auger scraper for expanded capability.

The dual-engine 627G is driven by a six-cylinder Cat 3406E EUI Diesel Engine, which features increased power in higher gear ranges. A 225-horsepower Cat 3306 DITA Diesel Engine powers the scraper. With its large fuel tank, the 627G stays in operation for 11 hours before refueling.
Caterpillar Inc.

This new addition to the Caterpillar Off-Highway Truck line, the 773E, has a payload capacity of 60 tons. Its 219,000-pound working weight is carried over a box-section frame, with nearly two dozen load-bearing castings built into high-stress areas. This relegates welds to lower-stress areas thereby boosting overall structural integrity. Information is gathered from all critical components of the 773E, including engine, drivetrain, and hydraulics, and fed to the operator station, where it is used to maximize productivity, monitor conditions, and plan maintenance.
Caterpillar Inc.

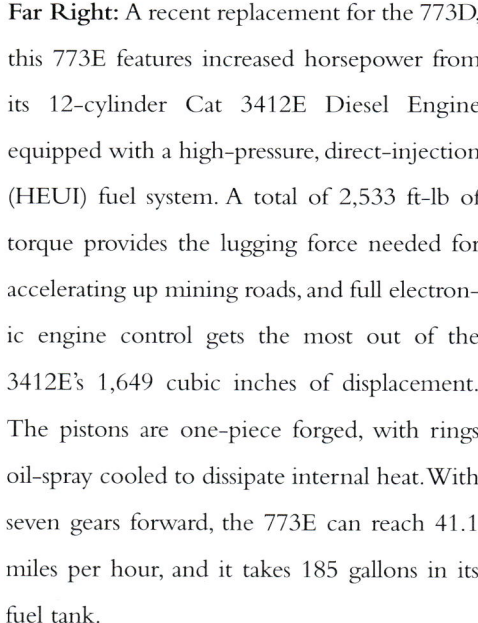

Far Right: A recent replacement for the 773D, this 773E features increased horsepower from its 12-cylinder Cat 3412E Diesel Engine equipped with a high-pressure, direct-injection (HEUI) fuel system. A total of 2,533 ft-lb of torque provides the lugging force needed for accelerating up mining roads, and full electronic engine control gets the most out of the 3412E's 1,649 cubic inches of displacement. The pistons are one-piece forged, with rings oil-spray cooled to dissipate internal heat. With seven gears forward, the 773E can reach 41.1 miles per hour, and it takes 185 gallons in its fuel tank.
Caterpillar Inc.

new cab designs with low profile front ends, giving the operators unsurpassed field of vision when the going gets tough. With their futuristic styling, they make a statement that Caterpillar not only builds some of the toughest articulated trucks available, but also some of the most stylish too.

The pillars of Caterpillar's product lines are still the classic and long running earth-moving machines, such as motor graders, scrapers, off-highway trucks, wheel loaders, and of coarse track-type tractors. Caterpillar offers no less than ten models of motor graders. Today's H-series machines, first introduced in late 1994, is the most compressive line up of motor graders available to the industry from a single manufacturer, led by such famous designs as the 12H, 14H, 16H, and 24H. The company's off-highway trucks often has the spotlight on its largest offering, the titanic 797B. But the quarry sized haulers are where the value truck orders are to be had. To keep pace with the competition, new E-series trucks started production in 2001. The first two of these improved quarry trucks are the 60-ton capacity 773E, and the 70-ton 775. For wheel loaders, the product line boasts 22 models, with the largest being the 994D. In late 2000, the company announced its new

988G Wheel Loader. Rated at 9.2 cubic yards, it is equipped with a mono boom design like that found on the 992G. As for the track-type tractors, dozers such as the D9R, D10R, and the massive D11R, have become legends in their own time. These dozers, along with the other 24 machines in the track-type tractor product line make up one of the finest and most productive dozers ever in the company's history, and are the true descendants of the Best and Holt legacy.

Except for the track-type tractors, nothing says Caterpillar more than the rather large and formidable wheel tractor-scrapers. With a heritage dating back to the early 1950s with the release of the DW21, Cat's wheel tractor-scraper line is the largest in the world. From the 15 cubic yard heaped model 611, to the 73 cubic yard heaped 657E Coal Bowl configuration, the wheel tractor-scrapers have over 50 years of experience on the job and counting. The latest releases are the G-series, starting in 2000. These include the 621G, the elevator

623G, and the twin-engined 627G. In 2001, the 631G, and 637G joined the group. As of 2003, the largest of Cat's wheel tractor-scrapers, the 651E and 657E, have yet to be released in a G-series configuration. As other manufacturers have let their scraper lines fall to the wayside, Caterpillar continues to build them. As wheel tractor-scrapers go, they are just about as close to perfection as a machine of this type will ever be. Though I would image there are a few Cat engineers that feel that they could be improved a bit more. That's the Caterpillar way.

We can only guess what the future of earthmoving holds. Given the company's successes in so many designs and applications, above and below terra firma, from fields to mines to the highways connecting our cities and towns, only the most productive and dependable machines in the world are worthy of wearing Caterpillar Yellow.

Pictured here are four Caterpillar G-Series Wheel Tractor-Scrapers. A dramatic improvement over the F series from the operator's perspective, G-Series wheel tractor-scrapers utilize enhanced stations and single-lever implement controls. The lone joystick replaces three levers in actuating virtually all implement movements, as well as the transmission hold and cushion hitch switches.
Caterpillar Inc.

A Caterpillar 988G Wheel Loader burdens its partner, a Caterpillar 773C Off-Highway Truck. The 475-horsepower wheel loader's 9.2 cubic yard bucket fills the hauler to its 60-ton capacity, which it can carry at speeds up to 41 miles per hour.
Caterpillar Inc.

THE NEXT CENTURY

Bench-loading articulated trucks with hydraulic excavators form an efficient earth-moving system used by many contractors. The Cat 385B Hydraulic Excavator shown is loading a Cat 740 Articulated Truck. The 385B has a 2.09 to 7.8 cubic yard heaped bucket capacity, while the 740 Articulated Truck has a 28.6 cubic yard heaped (SAE 2:1) capacity body.
Nick Cedar

The Caterpillar 637G is a tandem-powered wheel tractor-scraper with a Cat 3408E driving the tractor and a Cat 3306 DITA muscling the scraper. Its twin engines give it superior grading ability at steeper angles and in rougher conditions. The machine can be loaded under its own power or push-loaded with a Caterpillar D9 or D10. Like the 627G, two 637Gs can be configured in a push-pull arrangement for greater power and productivity.

Caterpillar Inc.

Caterpillar launched its popular backhoe loader line in 1985, quickly adding models including this 446 Backhoe Loader four years later. These incredibly versatile machines played an important role in the great residential housing boom of the 1990s. This one weighs 19,603 pounds, has a 1.5 cubic yard loader bucket and a 95-fly-wheel-horsepower engine.
Caterpillar Inc.

In 1999, Caterpillar introduced an entirely new line of skid steer loaders. These loaders were part of the company's new product lines of compact excavators and wheel loaders. The 236 is part of a family of ten skid steer models currently offered by the company. Power output of the 236 is 59 flywheel-horsepower.

Eric C. Orlemann

The Caterpillar 247 Multi-Terrain Loader is one of five different models introduced in 2001 featuring the ASV-built MTSS rubber-tracked undercarriage. The 247 is rated at 54 flywheel-horsepower, and can be equipped with a variety of bucket, fork, auger hammer, trencher, tiller, and broom attachments, meeting just about any type of job requirement a customer would require.
Eric C. Orlemann

This wheel tractor-scraper is configured with two 627Gs working together in a push-pull arrangement for high productivity. Each 627G is tandem-powered, so there are four Cat diesel engines at work on this job. The primary powerplant in each is the Cat 3406E, with six 5.4-inch-diameter cylinders, an 893 cubic inch displacement, which delivers 1,850 foot-pounds of torque at 1,200 rpm. The 627G is the first tandem-powered wheel tractor-scraper to offer scraper engine start-up and monitoring directly from the cab.
Caterpillar Inc.

INDEX

10-Ton, 34, 35
12H Motor Grader, 370
135H Motor Grader, 332
140H Motor Grader, 321
14D Motor Grader, 240
14H Motor Grader, 370
163H Motor Grader, 346, 347
16H Motor Grader, 340, 370
215 Excavator, 250
225 Excavator, 249, 250, 252–254
235 Excavator, 250
236 Skid Steer, 380
245 Excavator, 242, 243, 250, 292, 293
247 Multi-Terrain Loader, 381
24H Motor Grader, 325, 326, 341, 370
2-Ton, 34–36, 76, 77
30/30 Engineer Support Tractor, 284
314C Excavator, 344, 345
330B Log Loader, 356
330C Excavator, 314, 315
345BL Excavator, 345
350 Excavator, 318, 319
385B Excavator, 376
385BL Excavator, 357
436B Backhoe Loader, 317
446 Backhoe Loader, 378, 379
4x4 Ag Tractor, 282
5080 Excavator, 306
5090B Excavator, 306, 359
5110B Excavator, 310
5130 Excavator, 305, 306
5130B Excavator, 358
5230 Excavator, 310, 311, 316, 325
5-Ton, 34, 35, 110, 111
611 Wheel Tractor-Scraper, 372
613 Grader, 209
613 Wheel Tractor-Scraper, 194, 195
621 Wheel Tractor-Scraper, 206, 216, 217
621G Wheel Tractor-Scraper, 334, 367, 372, 373
623G Wheel Tractor-Scraper, 368, 373
627 Wheel Tractor-Scraper, 207
627F Wheel Tractor-Scraper, 261

627G Wheel Tractor-Scraper, 360, 361, 369, 373, 382
631B Wheel Tractor-Scraper, 202, 206, 239
631G Wheel Tractor-Scraper, 330, 331, 373
632 Wheel Tractor-Scraper, 202, 204
633 Wheel Tractor-Scraper, 208, 209, 260
637 Wheel Tractor-Scraper, 273
637G Wheel Tractor-Scraper, 366, 373, 377
641 Wheel Tractor-Scraper, 202, 207
650 Wheel Tractor-Scraper, 202, 204–206, 214, 215
651 Wheel Tractor-Scraper, 202
657 Wheel Tractor-Scraper, 202, 203, 209, 212, 213
657E Wheel Tractor-Scraper, 308, 309, 354, 372
660 Wheel Tractor-Scraper, 202, 204–206, 219
666 Wheel Tractor-Scraper, 202, 204–206, 218, 228, 229, 236, 237
725 Articulated Truck, 369
730 Articulated Truck, 369
735 Articulated Truck, 369
740 Articulated Truck, 364, 365, 369, 376
769, 176, 177, 192, 193, 249
772, 270, 271
773, 247, 249, 306, 307
773E Off-Highway Truck, 370, 371
775 Quarry Truck, 370
776 Off-Highway Tractor, 262–265
777 Off-Highway Truck, 249, 276, 277
777D Off-Highway Truck, 350
779 Rear Dump Truck, 244, 245, 248, 249
783 Articulated Truck, 232, 233, 244
785C Mining Truck, 316
786, 230, 231, 244
789B rear-dump hauler, 303, 306
793B Wheel Loader, 300, 301, 303, 304

793C Mining Truck, 304, 313, 320, 324
797 Off-Highway Truck, 313, 316-319, 322, 323, 351
797B Mining Truck, 334, 335, 370
824 Wheel Dozer, 180
825B Compactor, 180
830M tractor-dozer, 225
834 Wheel Dozer, 180, 238, 268, 269
835 Compactor, 180
844 tracked dozer, 343
844 Wheel Dozer, 329
854G Wheel Dozer, 172, 173, 329
920 Wheel Loader, 179
922 Wheel Loader, 175, 179, 180, 246
922A Traxcavator, 224
930 Wheel Loader, 179
933 Traxcavator, 245
941 Traxcavator, 245
944 Wheel Loader, 179
944A Traxcavator, 174–176, 198, 199
950 Wheel Loader, 179
951 Traxcavator, 245
951B track loader, 178, 179
955 Traxcavator, 245
955H track loader, 241
966A Wheel Loader, 175
966B Traxcavator, 176, 177
966G Wheel Loader, 284, 285, 311
973 track loader, 290, 291
977 Traxcavator, 245
980 Wheel Loader, 179, 286, 287
983 track loader, 180, 181, 294
983 Traxcavator, 246
988 Traxcavator, 176, 177, 251
988 Wheel Loader, 220, 221
988G Wheel Loader, 372, 374, 375
990 Wheel Loader, 310
992 Wheel Loader, 234, 272
992C Wheel Loader, 295, 304, 305
992G Wheel Loader, 298, 299, 326, 327, 329
994 Wheel Loader, 300, 302, 303, 312
994D Wheel Loader, 302, 339, 370

Auto Patrol motor grader, 118

Best 25, 68, 73
Best 30 Tracklayer, 30, 31, 34, 50, 51, 68, 69, 133
Best 40 Tracklayer, 30, 44–47, 49, 72, 73
Best 60 Tracklayer, 27, 30, 31, 33, 34, 48, 49, 56–59, 74, 75, 98, 99, 102, 103
Best 70 Tracklayer, 29
Best Combined Harvester, 8, 9
Best Steam Traction Engine No. 175, 19–21
Best Traction Engine, 8, 9, 11–13

Challenger 65, 282, 283
Challenger 70C, 282
Challenger 75, 282, 283
Challenger 85, 282, 283
Challenger 95E, 283
CS-563E Compactor, 348
CS-583E Compactor, 349

D10, 253, 254, 256, 257, 267, 296, 297, 372
D10N, 258
D10R, 257, 266
D11N, 257–259, 274, 275
D11R Carrydozer, 320–325, 355, 372
D11R Track-Type Tractor, 259, 319-325, 336, 337, 352, 353
D2, 100, 101, 126, 127, 135, 139, 190, 200
D20D Articulated Truck, 281
D22 Articulated Truck, 281
D25 Articulated Truck, 281
D25C Articulated Truck, 278, 279
D275 Articulated Truck, 281
D300B Articulated Truck, 281
D30C Articulated Truck, 281
D330 Articulated Truck, 281
D35 Articulated Truck, 281
D350 Articulated Truck, 281

D4, 116, 117, 127, 137, 139, 164, 165, 190, 191
D400 Articulated Truck, 280, 281
D40D Articulated Truck, 281
D44B Articulated Truck, 281
D5, 127
D550 Articulated Truck, 281
D5N, 342
D6, 116, 117, 127, 128, 130, 139, 156, 157
D7, 116, 117, 128, 139, 144–146, 166–169
D7E, 196, 197
D7R, 344
D8, 116, 117, 147, 160, 161, 166, 167, 174–176, 189, 196, 197, 223
D8D, 197
D8E, 197
D8F, 197
D8G, 197
D8H, 197, 222, 255, 258
D8N, 328, 329
D8R, 333, 334
D9, 196–198, 201, 226, 227, 251
D9D, 188, 197, 200
D9E, 198
D9G, 198, 253, 259
D9H, 198, 245
D9L, 288, 289
D9N, 257
D9R dozer, 372
D9X, 197
DD9G tandem tractor, 212
DD9H tandem tractor, 213
DEployable Universal Combat Earthmover (DEUCE), 284, 285
Diesel Auto Patrol motor grader, 118, 119
Diesel Fifty, 88, 89
Diesel Forty, 86, 127
Diesel No. 10 Auto Patrol motor grader, 121
Diesel No. 10 motor grader, 119
Diesel No. 11 Auto Patrol motor grader, 121
Diesel No. 11 motor grader, 119
Diesel No. 12 Auto Patrol motor grader, 119, 121, 150, 151
Diesel Seventy, 90, 93, 97, 102
Diesel Seventy-Five, 80, 81, 93, 96
Diesel Sixty, 62, 63, 83–87, 90, 110, 114

Diesel Sixty-Five, 90, 94, 95
Diesel Thirty-Five, 86, 134, 135
DJB D250 Articulated Truck, 281
DJB D44 Articulated Truck, 281
Drott Tractor Loader, 125
DW10, 132, 133, 148, 149
DW15, 132
DW20, 133–136, 183
DW21 Wheel Tractor-Scraper, 186, 372
DW21, 133, 135, 136

Fifteen, 36, 38, 118, 125
Fifty, 86–89
Forty, 86, 122

Holt 10-Ton, 22, 23, 32–35, 54, 55
Holt 120, 26, 27, 29
Holt 18 Midget, 24, 25, 43, 56, 66, 67
Holt 2-Ton, 22, 23, 31, 52, 53, 75
Holt 40, 24, 38–43
Holt 45, 24, 25, 29, 30, 78, 79
Holt 5-Ton, 22, 23, 31, 32, 36, 37
Holt 60, 25, 26, 51, 64, 65
Holt 75, 26, 27–31
Holt Baby 30, 24, 25
Holt Junior Road Engine, 11
Holt Junior Steam Traction Engine No. 77, 12, 14, 15, 18
Holt Senior Road Engine, 11
Holt Standard Road Engine, 11
Holt Steamer Road Engine, 16, 17
Holt T-29, 32, 33
Holt Traction Engine, 11–13

J619 Wheel Tractor-Scraper, 207, 208

LeTourneau Angledozer, 145, 160, 166, 167
LeTourneau Knockdown Bulldozer Blade, 161
LeTourneau LS Carryall Scraper, 149, 165–167
LeTourneau Tournapull, 125

MDW8, 139

No. 10 Auto Patrol Motor Grader, 121, 128, 129
No. 10 Motor Grader, 118
No. 10 scraper, 128, 133
No. 100 Auto Patrol Motor Grader, 162, 163
No. 11 Auto Patrol Motor Grader, 121, 152–155
No. 112 Motor Grader, 121, 199
No. 12 Motor Grader, 121, 199
No. 120 Motor Grader, 199
No. 14 Motor Grader, 199
No. 15 scraper, 133
No. 16 Motor Grader, 199–201, 204, 205
No. 20 terracer, 130
No. 21 scraper, 135
No. 212 Motor Grader, 121
No. 22 Pull Grader, 136
No. 27 Cable Control, 136
No. 28 scraper, 128
No. 35 Pull Grader, 135
No. 4 Motor Patrol Motor Grader, 122, 123
No. 40 pull-scraper, 116, 117
No. 40 scraper, 128, 131
No. 456 scraper, 135, 136, 183
No. 46 Hydraulic Control, 136
No. 470 scraper, 135
No. 48 grader, 170, 171
No. 6 Traxcavator Shovel, 139
No. 60 pull-scraper, 116, 117, 128, 130, 131, 189
No. 66 grader, 86, 90
No. 668C Wheel Tractor, 136, 186
No. 668S bulldozer blade, 136
No. 7 Auto Patrol Motor Grader, 126, 127
No. 7 Motor Grader, 118
No. 70 pull-scraper, 116, 117, 128, 130, 131, 189
No. 80 pull-scraper, 116, 117, 128, 130, 131, 189
No. 9 Auto Patrol Motor Grader, 124
No. 9 Motor Grader, 118
No. 90 scraper, 116, 117, 128, 130, 131

Peterson Quad-Trac D9G, 211–213, 235–237

R1700, 362, 363
R-2, 121, 122
R-3, 115, 121, 122
R-4, 39, 121, 122, 132
R-5, 121, 122
RD-4, 127
RD-6, 127, 138, 139
RD-7, 128, 142, 143
RD-8, 170, 171, 196, 197
Russell Motor Hi-Way Patrol, 118, 119

Seventy, 90, 91, 102, 104–109
Sixty, 27, 30, 34, 35, 49, 60, 61, 74, 75, 82, 98, 99, 102, 103
Sixty-Five, 90, 92, 93
SxS D9G bulldozer, 213
SxS D9H, 250

T7 Traxcavator, 158, 159
Tandem 657, 208
Ten, 36, 38, 70, 71, 118
Thirty, 34, 35, 122, 133, 137
Thirty-Five, 86, 122, 135
Tiger 690A Wheel Dozer, 329
Trackson Traxcavator T2, 139, 190
Trackson Traxcavator T4, 139, 190
Trackson Traxcavator T6, 139
Trackson Traxcavator T7, 139
Traxcavator HT4, 139, 190, 191
Traxcavator LW2, 139
Traxcavator MD6, 139
Traxcavator MD7, 139
Traxcavator MD8, 139
Traxcavator PD4, 139
Traxcavator T4, 139
Traxcavator T6, 139
Traxcavator T7, 139
Traxcavator TracLoader L2, 139
Triple 657 Wheel Tractor-Scraper, 208, 210, 211
Twenty, 39, 112, 118
Twenty-Eight, 39, 118, 122, 131
Twenty-Five, 39, 113
Twenty-Two, 39, 130